S0-FAE-286

ODELL GRIFFIN

THE
RAPTURE
PUZZLE

BIBLICALLY PUTTING
THE PIECES TOGETHER

Outskirts Press, Inc.
Denver, Colorado

The opinions expressed in this manuscript are solely the opinions of the author and do not represent the opinions or thoughts of the publisher. The author represents and warrants that s/he either owns or has the legal right to publish all material in this book.

The Rapture Puzzle
Biblically Putting the Pieces Together
All Rights Reserved.
Copyright © 2008 Odell Griffin
V2.0

This book may not be reproduced, transmitted, or stored in whole or in part by any means, including graphic, electronic, or mechanical without the express written consent of the publisher except in the case of brief quotations embodied in critical articles and reviews.

Outskirts Press, Inc.
http://www.outskirtspress.com

ISBN: 978-1-4327-1851-0

Outskirts Press and the 'OP' logo are trademarks belonging to Outskirts Press, Inc.

PRINTED IN THE UNITED STATES OF AMERICA

Table of Contents

Introduction

The purpose of this book is to illuminate through Scripture what the Bible says about the timing of the rapture. My goal is for this book to be a guide using Scripture in context, comparing Scripture with Scripture, and examining the Bible to see what Scripture actually says, not what someone says it says.

I have been interested in the study of end times for many years. Looking back, I realize that all my teachers held the pre-tribulation rapture view. In general, the pre-tribulation rapture view holds that Christ could return and remove (rapture) the church from earth 'at any moment' with no needed fulfillment of prophetic events or signs. During the time that I believed the pre-tribulation view, I would read Scriptures at face value and then be told that what I was reading did not mean what I thought it meant. For example, I would be told that a particular Scripture did not apply to the church, even though it read as though it should apply to the church. I remember that I thought this was strange, but did not question it. Soon I was interpreting the end-time Scriptures in the way others guided me, instead of the most natural understanding.

The pre-tribulation rapture view that I was taught is the most popular view in this country and relates to the beliefs that the *Left Behind* series is based. On the surface, this view is very convincing and appears to be a solid teaching. Yet, when I took a closer look, I saw flaws.

In this book I share with you what changed my mind from being a believer in the pre-tribulation rapture to being a believer in the pre-wrath rapture view. The pre-wrath rapture view holds that there are signs and events that must occur before Christ returns to remove (rapture) the true church. On the surface, this may not sound like a major issue, but it is. I am grateful to Marvin Rosenthal who wrote *The Pre-Wrath Rapture of the Church*, Robert Van Kampen, who wrote *The Sign*, and Bible teacher Charles Cooper for revealing what the Scriptures have always said about the rapture, the coming of the Lord, and the signs associated with it. These men have used sound interpretation principles in comparing Scripture with Scripture, and they have done it in context. They left no stone unturned. I invite you to read this book, and I encourage you to look at the Scriptures in context and then draw your own conclusion as to what the Scriptures really say.

Notes to the Reader

In this book, I will be comparing the pre-tribulation rapture view with the pre-wrath rapture view. One of my writing goals was to make a book that could be enjoyed by a wide range of readers. I want beginners in this subject to be able to gain knowledge from reading this book, and I want advanced scholars to be challenged by the concepts in this book.

For Beginners and Intermediates: I want you to enjoy this book. Chapter two is specifically for beginners and intermediates who do not have a wide range of knowledge about the end times. It gives a simple overview of end-time events. After reading chapters one and two, you will have a grasp on the main events of the end times. Then you can continue to read the book in sequence or you can go to specific chapters of interest. Moreover, I have repeated some concepts numerous times so that you can firmly grasp certain key concepts. If you come across a term that you need defined, there is a glossary in the back of the book.

For Advanced Students of Scripture: I realize that you may have certain specific Scriptural passages of interest. I have arranged this book so that you do not have to read it in the order it is presented. If you have a firm grasp on the end times Scriptures and understand the fundamentals of pre-tribulation and pre-wrath, you can start with any chapter and be challenged to think deeply about the content.

As the title of this book suggests (*The Rapture Puzzle*), each chapter literally contains pieces of the rapture puzzle. When putting a puzzle together, the pieces are compared with the picture on the box to be more easily assembled. In *The Rapture Puzzle*, we will carefully compare Scripture in context with Scripture to get a more complete picture of end-time events and their timing. Many charts (that compare Scripture with Scripture) are used throughout this book to assist you in getting a mental picture of what different passages of Scripture are telling us and where they belong on a time line of the end times.

Chapter 1

Basic Views of the End Times

The teaching or study concerning the end times is called *eschatology*. The Greek word *eschatos* means *last* or *final*. It is the study of the end times. In this chapter, we will give a simple overview of different views about the end times and their definitions. We will focus on the most popular view held in the United States and compare it to Scripture while highlighting the end-time view that I have found to be the one that truly follows the Scriptural picture of the end times.

As you work your way through this book, you will develop a solid biblical understanding of the end-time events and you will be prepared to discuss biblically the end of the age, the day of the Lord (the future time when God's wrath is poured out on the wicked on earth), the 70th week of Daniel (a future seven-year period when the final end-time events unfold, [also referred to as the tribulation]), the great tribulation (begins at the midpoint of the 70th week of Daniel [also known as the tribulation], when the antichrist begins his persecution of the nation of Israel and all who truly follow Christ), and other terms comparing Scripture with Scripture. I have included a unique time-line chart that compares Scripture from the books of Revelation, Matthew, Mark, Luke, 1 &

2 Thessalonians, and Daniel. You will see how each book is related and be able to put a time frame on key Scriptures.

If you know very little about the end times, the first three chapters will lay a foundation and give you a basic understanding of general time lines and basic definitions. If you already have an understanding of the end times, the first three chapters will be a refresher for you. You will see many Greek and Hebrew words in *italics* throughout this book. There will be a Strong's number in parentheses next to the Greek or Hebrew word. This is literally the number assigned to the word in a *Strong's Complete Word Study Concordance*. If you have a *Strong's Concordance*, it will assist you in your study. I have also provided a list of all the Greek and Hebrew words used throughout this book. This list also contains the Strong's number and basic definitions of each word. Most people are not concerned about Greek words. If that is the case with you, ignore the Greek word and the Strong's number, but do look at the meaning. It will deepen your understanding.

Many who study the end times would agree that there is a seven-year period that is to come and most will call it the tribulation period. It is agreed that the time will be a time of great distress and persecution for the inhabitants of the earth. The Greek word for *tribulation* is *thlipsis* (Strong's #2347), which literally means *pressure*; great pressure will be applied to those who do not submit to the world leader to come, who the Bible calls 'the antichrist, the beast, the man of sin or the son of perdition.' It is important to note that Jesus said this period of tribulation would be cut short (Matt. 24:22). This does not mean that the seven-year period will be shortened, but that the worldwide persecution of believers will be shortened. (We will deal with this in detail later.) The Bible also teaches that there will be a time when the church or faithful followers of Jesus Christ will be removed from the earth at the return (second coming) of Christ, before God's wrath is poured out on earth, since believers are not appointed to God's wrath (1 Thess. 4:15-17; 1 Cor. 15:50-53; Rom. 5:9; 1 Thess. 5:9). This future removal of believers from the earth is what is most commonly referred to as the *rapture* of the church. (Although the word *rapture* is not found in Scripture, this event is clearly taught.

It comes from the Latin word *raptus*, meaning a *carrying or taking away*.)

Millennial Views

The term *Millennium* comes from the Latin word *mille*, meaning *a thousand* referring to the 1000-year reign of Christ and His saints mentioned in Revelation 20:4-6. A thousand years is mentioned six times in the first seven verses of that chapter. During this thousand-year period, Satan will be bound. In other words, he will have no personal influence on creation while Christ reigns on earth. There are three general views related to the millennium. They are all related to the timing of Christ's return and when His 1000-year reign will begin. They are identified by prefixes (pre-, post-, and a-). The *pre-millennial view* holds that Christ will return *before* (*pre*) His millennial kingdom is established here on earth. He will return and defeat the enemies of God before He begins His earthly rule. This is called *pre-millennialism*. The pre-millennial view is the view that this author holds.

The *post-millennial* view holds that Christ will return after (post) the millennial kingdom is established. In general, they believe that the church, through spreading the gospel, will cause the world to get increasingly better until the righteous control the world and evil will literally be removed. Then Christ will return to earth to reign. This is called *post-millennialism*.

The last view is the *amillennial view*. The prefix *a-* means *no or not*. The amillennial view holds that there will be no literal thousand-year period. It is a symbolic expression that should be spiritualized. They believe that Christ reigns in the present spiritual life of believers. This is called *amillennialism*.

So we have found that the *pre-millennial view* states that Christ will return *before* the millennium. The *post-millennial view* states that Christ will return *after* the millennium, and the *amillennial view* states that there *will not* be a literal 1000-year reign of Christ.

Rapture Views

Just like the millennial views, there are three rapture views that use prefixes to identify their belief about the timing of the rapture. These prefixes (*pre-, mid-,* and *post-*) usually precede the word *tribulation*. There is a fourth view that precedes the word *wrath*. It is called *pre-wrath*. The understanding of the timing of God's wrath is key for a proper understanding of the timing of the rapture. It is also important to understand what *is* and what is *not* God's wrath. An improper understanding of what God's wrath is and its timing will lead to an improper view of the rapture.

PRE-TRIBULATION RAPTURE

There are those who believe that this entire future seven-year period (the 70th week of Daniel) is God's wrath. Since they hold this view, they believe that the church will be removed (raptured) from earth before this seven-year period of tribulation begins. This is called the *pre-tribulation rapture view. Pre* meaning *before*, and tribulation, speaking of this period of persecution and pressure. The pre-tribulation view is the most widely held and taught view in the United States today. It is argued passionately by many believers and is the view of the popular *Left Behind* series.

MID-TRIBULATION RAPTURE

Some Christians believe that only half of this seven-year period is God's wrath. They believe that the church will be raptured (removed from the earth) at the three and a half year point in the tribulation, when the Bible says the Great Tribulation will begin (Matt. 24:15-21; Dan. 9:27). This is called the *Mid-tribulation rapture view*. *Mid* meaning the *middle*, and tribulation is speaking of this period of persecution and pressure.

POST-TRIBULATION RAPTURE

POST-TRIBULATION RAPTURE

God's Wrath	
Tribulation	The Great Tribulation
3 - 1/2 Years	3 - 1/2 Years
THE 70TH WEEK OF DANIEL – 7 YEAR PERIOD	

Yet, there is another group who believes that the church will be removed after the seven-year period ends. This is called the *Post-tribulation rapture view*. *Post* meaning *after*, and tribulation, referring to the period of persecution and pressure. Those who hold the Post-tribulation view generally believe that the church will be kept from God's wrath by protection while remaining on earth.

It is obvious that what view you hold depends on your view about when God's wrath actually begins. The major rapture argument is about timing. Timing is everything. Those that hold the pre-tribulation view believe that the rapture is imminent. By their definition of imminent, they mean that it can happen at any moment without a sign. Is this what the Bible teaches? We will see what the Scriptures say later in the book.

Each of these views is argued vigorously among believers. Each view has its strengths and weaknesses. Each view claims to be biblically accurate. But, there can only be one view that can truly make the claim that it represents the truth revealed in Scripture.

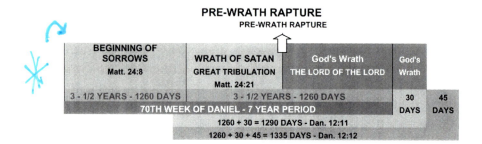

PRE-WRATH RAPTURE

There is another view that is called the *Pre-wrath rapture view*. It is called *pre-wrath* because it holds that the followers of Jesus Christ (the true church) will be removed from earth (raptured) *before* God's wrath begins. On the surface, it may sound like the pre-tribulation or mid-tribulation view. However, the difference is that the pre-wrath rapture view emphasizes that the true church will be raptured during the great tribulation (persecution) of the antichrist. This will occur sometime *after* the midpoint of the 70th week of Daniel, but sometime before the end of the 70th week of Daniel. The great tribulation, which begins at the midpoint of the 70th week of Daniel, is called Satan's wrath. The great tribulation is not God's wrath. There is a major biblical difference between Satan's wrath (the great tribulation) and God's wrath (the day of the Lord). During the great tribulation, only the righteous will be persecuted, but during God's wrath, only the wicked will be persecuted. During the great tribulation, the antichrist will be exalted (2 Thess. 2:3-4), but during God's wrath, only the Lord will be exalted (Is. 2:11, 17). It is biblically impossible for these two events to go on at the same time. It is God's wrath that believers are not appointed to. The great tribulation will be cut short by the Second coming of Christ, which occurs at the rapture. At that time, the wrath of God will begin to be poured out on the wicked world. This event will occur after the sixth seal, but before the seventh seal of Revelation. There are signs associated with these events. The *pre-wrath rapture* view most accurately reflects the belief of the early first and second-century believers. In studying this view, I believe that it most accurately divides the word of God concerning the end times. It correctly explains the timing of the rapture, God's wrath (the day of the Lord), and even Satan's wrath (the great tribulation). It also accurately reflects the repeated biblical theme that, at the second coming of Christ (when God's wrath will begin on earth) the righteous will be rescued and the wicked will be punished.

Something to Think About

The views presented in this chapter are meant to give the basic views of the end times. Nevertheless, there are some who hold a historical view of the book of Revelation and other prophetic verses. This means they believe that the information that I am presenting as end-time events are not end-time events, but are things that have happened in the past. I must say that I believe that many of the prophecy events mentioned in Scripture were written to warn the first-century church of events that would occur in their day; however, I do not believe that it stops there. Let us not forget that throughout the Bible, we can find near-far prophecies. By near-far, I mean that a prophetic event can have a fulfillment at the time that the prophetic statement was made (near) and a fulfillment in the distant future (far).

Since it is not uncommon for near-far prophecies to occur in Scripture, we should not be skeptical about seeing the fulfillment of one during future end-time events. Looking back at past events will allow us to get a glimpse of what is to come. Chapter 11 in this book contains some of the views of the church fathers who lived after first-century believers. They clearly believed that end-time events were still yet future.

Face Value Hermeneutics (Finding the Truth)

Scholars disagree on the correct interpretation of different passages in the Bible. There are numerous opinions. Yet, the Bible is not the problem. The problem is with man and his hermeneutics (method of interpretation). Without adhering to the proper guidelines for Biblical interpretation, a person can easily fall into interpreting a verse based on his or her personal view. Therefore, it is important to mention some basic guidelines for studying the Bible.

There is an art to studying the Bible. Finding the complete truth should always be the goal. A. W. Tozer said, 'When you find the truth of Scripture, that truth always stands in judgment of you; you never stand in judgment of it.' Ultimately, the best study guide for the Bible is the Bible itself. There are no contradictions in the Bible. Therefore, if you find what you believe to be an apparent contradiction, you must keep searching. You do not yet have the complete truth.

There are many books and resources on how to study the Bible. A good DVD on the subject is 'Pursuing Truth' by Charles Cooper. The book *Knowing Scripture* by R. C. Sproul is an excellent choice. Note that the remainder of this chapter is based on a very concise book (only 24 pages) on the subject called *Understanding Scripture at Face Value* by Robert Van Kampen and Charles Cooper.

There are basic rules to use as we read and understand a document. These basic rules are called hermeneutics. Hermeneutics is an important subject in the Christian faith. We use it every day. We use it when we read books, magazines, newspapers, and any type of reading that requires a certain amount of interpretation. However, when it comes to the Bible, there is an art of (biblical) interpretation required. Biblical Hermeneutics (interpretation) has general and special rules. The first thing that we must realize is that there are historical, linguistic (language and grammar), and cultural differences from the time that Scripture was written to today. Therefore, our goal is to determine what the original author meant when it was written.

There are two broad over-arching methods or approaches to interpreting and understanding the Bible. One is the Allegorical Method, which means that the literal words are not what the text actually means. This creates a major problem, because it is very subjective. Using this method allows the reader to *determine* what he or she wants it to mean. This allows readers to make a passage of Scripture mean anything they want it to mean. This can lead to heretical (an opinion contrary to Bible truth) teaching. Therefore, the allegorical method of biblical interpretation should be rejected. Ultimately, any method that does not attempt to discover the normal, natural, customary sense of the text is using an allegorical interpretation.

The second broad over-arching method is called the Literal or Face Value Method. It is a face-value method of reading that takes all of the rules of interpretation into consideration. These rules include grammar, history, figures of speech, theology, and genre (the type of writing or literature). Using this method, the reader *discovers* what the Scripture means. This method is both objective and subjective. The attempt in this method is to discover the most normal, natural, customary meaning of any text while remembering that there are different types of figures of speech. The face-value method is obviously the preferred method of biblical interpretation. As you can imagine, your hermeneutics determines your interpretation, so it is important to get it right.

Five Principles for Scripture Study

1. Seek to discover the author's intended meaning. 'All Scripture *is* given by inspiration of God' – 2 Timothy 3:16a NKJV. The meaning of a passage is *determined* by the author and *discovered* by the reader. The intended meaning never changes. I have heard it put this way: If the plain sense makes sense, you have the right sense. A passage of Scripture will have one *interpretation* that the author meant at the time of writing; however, it can have many *applications*. Yet, a passage may mean more than the author understood, because God intended more that the human author understood (Joel 2:28-32 vs. Acts 2:17-21). By *interpretation*, I mean what specifically the author was intending to convey or communicate to his reader at the time of the writing. By *application*, I mean how a

particular passage of Scripture can apply to the reader's life at different times and situations.

2. Recognize the importance of context. Context may be the most important interpretive principle in the face value method. The Bible is made of books, chapters, paragraphs, sentences, phrases, and words. To discover the meaning of an individual word, we must look at its context within a phrase, sentence, paragraph, chapter, or book. We must also keep in mind, to whom is the author speaking. What genre (type of writing or literature) is it? Remember that the context limits what a word *can* mean. Context offers clues. A text without context is a pretext. By that I mean that a passage of Scripture can mean anything that the reader wants it to mean when taken out of context. The reader can literally make the Bible say whatever he or she chooses to believe (right or wrong). For example, in the English language today, if a person says, 'he got burned,' it is the context that determines what it actually means. If the context is at a track meet, he was simply outrun. If the context is some type of fire, he was physically burned. In the business world, it would mean that he got the short end of a stick. Another phrase that requires context.

3. Let Scripture interpret Scripture. There are no contradictions in the Bible. Interpret difficult passages with passages of clear meaning. 'The entirety of Your word is truth.' - Psalm 119:160a NKJV. As Martin Luther said, 'The best interpreter of Scripture is other Scripture!'

4. Determine the literal reference of figures of speech. Remember that even though the Bible should be read and understood at face value, it still uses *figures of speech* just like we do today. These figures of speech can be used for comparison, substitution, or amplification. Face value hermeneutics recognizes figures of speech. This is extremely important. Some

forms of figures of speech are similes, metaphors, idioms, metonymies, and parallelism.

- *Similes* make direct comparisons. We find connecting words such as *like* or *as*. For example (from Revelation 1:14 KJV emphasis added), 'His head and his hairs were white *like* wool, *as* white *as* snow; and his eyes were *as* a flame of fire.'
- *Metaphors* use an implied comparison rather than a direct comparison. Revelation 12:4b KJV states, '...the dragon stood before the woman which was ready to be delivered, for to devour her child as soon as it was born.' To find out who or what the dragon is, we must look elsewhere in Scripture. Revelation 12:9a KJV states, 'And the great dragon was cast out, that old serpent, called the Devil, and Satan.' We find that the dragon is actually Satan, the Devil.
- *Idioms* are expressions.
- *Metonymy* is a substitution. Psalm 23:5 KJV states, 'Thou preparest a table before me in the presence of mine enemies: thou anointest my head with oil; my cup runneth over.' The word *table* means *feast*.
- *Parallelism* is a form of amplification. We usually find this in poetry (Psalm and Proverbs). An idea is stated, and then it is clarified or amplified with addition information.

5. Look for near/far implications and applications in prophetic passages, such as the seven churches of Revelation. This is specific to prophecy alone. This does not mean that Scripture has two meanings.

Chapter 2

Easy Overview of Pre-Wrath Rapture View

This chapter will give readers a quick survey of the main points in the pre-wrath view. The following chapters will take certain key aspects of the debate between pre-wrath and pre-tribulation and allow you to investigate the facts for yourself.

The Main Difference Between the Two Views

It is clear in Scripture that believers are not appointed to God's wrath (1 Thess. 5:9; Rom. 5:9). So, both the pre-tribulation rapture view and the pre-wrath rapture view agree that the rapture occurs before God's wrath. However, they disagree about what God's wrath *is* and as to *when* God's wrath begins. The pre-tribulation rapture view says that God's wrath will begin at the beginning of the 70th week of Daniel (the final seven-year period on the earth before the beginning of the millennium). The pre-wrath rapture view separates Satan's wrath from God's wrath. During Satan's wrath, only the righteous are persecuted, but during God's wrath, only the wicked are persecuted. Pre-wrath says that the first 3 ½ years of the last seven-year period is a time of increasing turmoil on the earth. Then at the midpoint of the seven-year period, Satan's wrath (the great tribulation) begins. At some point God will bring Satan's wrath to an end by the rapture of the church at the second coming of Christ. God's wrath (the day of the Lord) will then be poured out on earth. Therefore the pre-wrath rapture view says that the rapture occurs after Satan's wrath - meaning that the church will go through Satan's wrath (the great tribulation). After the rapture, God's wrath will begin. So the name *pre-wrath* means 'before God's wrath.'

The Basic Beliefs of the Pre-Wrath View

When the earth comes to the final seven years talked about in Daniel 9:27, the world will enter a time known as the beginning of sorrows (Matt. 24:8). Earthly disasters (such as wars, earthquakes, and famines) will increase. As we approach the middle of the seven years, the antichrist will emerge as a world leader. He will gain the allegiance of the unbelievers. In the middle of the seven years, he will enter the temple of the Jews* and will commit a terrible sin. It is called the abomination of desolation. It is thought that he will sit on a throne in the temple and call himself God.

On the day that the antichrist enters the temple and does this terrible sin, persecution of the Christians and Jews begins in full force. The Bible tells all who are in Judea to run and escape out of Jerusalem into the hills (Matt. 24:15-21). This time is called the great tribulation (Satan's wrath). Satan will exalt himself above all others.

The antichrist will cause everyone to get a mark in his or her hand or forehead. This mark is an identification that gives people the right to get food and supplies to live. It is a mark of dedication to the antichrist (and essentially to Satan). All those who will not give their allegiance to the antichrist will be killed or imprisoned. There will be many Christians jailed and killed, because they will not take the mark.

At some point, God will create tremendous cosmic

disturbances, and the sun, moon, and stars will not be seen. Darkness will fall on the earth. That is the sign that the rapture is imminent. Then suddenly, bright light occurs and the church is raptured. Angels will gather all believers from on earth and in heaven to meet Jesus Christ in the air. The graves are opened, freeing the bodies of the dead in Christ. The spirits of the dead in Christ come from heaven to meet their new glorified bodies in the air along with Christ and their loved ones in Christ. Those who are alive are changed and receive glorified bodies immediately, also joining in the glorious reunion. The church is taken to their home in heaven for an unimaginable feast.

The day of the Lord, also called God's wrath, begins when the rapture occurs. God begins to pour out His judgment on the earth. Horrible events take place such as 1/3 of the sea is destroyed, 1/3 of the rivers become bitter, and terrible locusts are released that torment the unbelievers. God's wrath is associated with the trumpet and bowl judgments.

Among the events in the last 3 ½ years, two Jewish witnesses will prophesy on earth until the end of the seven-year period. After 3 ½ years, they are killed by the antichrist, lie dead for 3 ½ days, and then before the eyes of the world, they are resurrected and ascend to heaven.

The Battle of Armageddon is the last military confrontation on the earth. Armies of the earth gather to make war against Christ and His army. Christ will destroy the armies of the earth. The antichrist and the false prophet will be cast alive into the lake of fire burning with brimstone. Therefore, the antichrist and his armies will be totally annihilated. Satan will then be bound and cast into the bottomless pit. He will remain there for a thousand years. All people who followed the antichrist and false prophet will have a final judgment of hell (separation from God for eternity).

All those who have become believers since the rapture (the Jewish converts to Christ) and any others who survived will enter the Millennial Kingdom. The Bible seems to indicate there will be a few Gentiles who believe after the rapture. The Millennium is a thousand-year period in which Jesus Christ reigns over the earth. Those who entered the millennium will continue to live life in a similar way as before except they will live it as believers in Jesus Christ. After one thousand years, Satan is released and there is a final confrontation. Satan loses the conflict and is thrown into the lake of fire. The Great White Throne Judgment (the judgment for the lost) will begin. All who are lost and whose names are not written in the *Book of Life* will receive their judgment here. They will be cast into the lake of fire. Then righteous will dwell forever in the new heaven and new earth. This is eternity!

*The temple of the Jews in Jerusalem will probably be rebuilt. There is an organization in Jerusalem that already has manufactured the temple furniture and supplies. They are planning the rebuilding of the temple. Nevertheless, it could be a temple much like the temple in the wilderness during the time of Moses.

Chapter 3

Daniel's Time Line of the End Times

The purpose of this chapter is to give a basic understanding of Daniel's seventy-week prophecy, the 70th week of Daniel, and the time line associated with it. I will not go into great detail about Daniel's prophecy, but will provide a general overview. The Daniel that I am speaking of is the same Daniel who was thrown in the lions' den. He wrote the book of Daniel, which is in the Old Testament. You will also find the story of Shadrach, Meshach, and Abed-Nego in the book of Daniel. If you are going to study the end times, you will need to have some type of understanding of what Daniel has written. The key chapters concerning prophecy (in the book of Daniel) are 9, 10, 11, and 12. The book of Daniel holds the key to the timeline of prophetic events. Jesus Himself specifically mentioned Daniel's prophecy concerning the abomination of desolation in the passages in the New Testament that we now call the Olivet Discourse (Matt. 24:15; Mark 13:14). Jesus thereby legitimizes Daniel's prophecy and ties it to the Olivet Discourse.

What's a Week?

In Daniel 9:24-27, we will see a prophecy of seventy weeks, which is usually called the Seventy Weeks of Daniel. When we hear the word *week* in English, we think of seven days. However, in Hebrew, a week is a seven, but not necessarily seven days. It actually means *seven*. So technically, it could be called 'Seventy-Sevens.' The context in which it is used will determine what is being counted—much like the word *dozen*. When using the word *dozen*, the context in which it is used will determine what is being counted. It could be a dozen eggs, people, or years. In the context of Daniel chapter 9, a week is seven years. So, *one week (one seven-year period)* would be 1 x 7 = 7 years. *Seven weeks (seven seven-year periods)* would be 7 x 7 = 49 years and *sixty-two weeks* would be 62 x 7 = 434 years. Adding them all together would be seventy weeks or in other words 490 years (1 week + 7 weeks + 62 weeks = 70 weeks [7 + 49 + 434 = 490 years]). The prophecy is broken up in precisely these amounts of time. Sixty-nine of these weeks (483 year period of time) have been fulfilled; however, there is still one week (7 year period of time) to be fulfilled in the future to complete this prophecy. It is called the 70th week of Daniel. Throughout this book, you will find the phrase 'the 70th week of Daniel.' Just know that the 70th week means a seven-year period of time. Some call this period of time the 7-year tribulation period, or just the tribulation. We will see later in Scripture how Jesus broke this 7-year period up and what He actually called it. Understanding this is key to an accurate scriptural view of what is to come and who will be affected.

Confirming and Breaking the Covenant

The confirming of a seven-year covenant between the antichrist and the nation of Israel will mark the beginning of the 70th week of Daniel (Dan. 9:27a). The world may or may not know when this covenant is confirmed; nevertheless, it will mark the beginning of this 7-year period. However, at the midpoint of this period, the covenant is broken by the antichrist and the abomination of desolation will occur (Dan. 9:27b). The antichrist will desecrate the temple and begin his persecution of the nation of Israel, the followers of Christ, and anyone who does not submit to the rule of the antichrist (Dan. 12:1; Matt. 24:9,15-21; Rev. 12:13-17; 13:7,15-17).

Three and a Half Years (3 ½ years)

In Scripture, you will see the terms *time, times, and half a time* (Dan. 12:7; Rev. 12:14), '1260 days' (Rev. 11:3; 12:6), and '42 months' (Rev. 13:5). Each of these terms refers to a 3 ½-year period of time, more specifically the final 3 ½ years of the 70th week of Daniel. These terms are broken down as follows:

- *Time, times, and half a time:* The term *time* literally means *one year*. The term *times* means *two years*, which would mean that *a half of time* would mean *a half-year* (6 months). So, adding them together would make 3 ½ years (one year + two years + a half-year).
- *1260 days*: There are 360 days in a prophetic year, which would make 180 days in a prophetic half-year. So, 360 days x 3 = 1080 days. If you add 180 days to 1080 days, you get *1260 days*. So, prophetically speaking, 1260 days is 3 ½ years.
- *42 months:* We all know that there are 12 months in a year. So, 12 months x 3 = 36 months, which is 3 years. If you add 6 months to it, you get 42 months, which of course is 3 ½ years.

You will also see a term in Scripture called the *midst* or *middle of the week* (Dan. 9:27b). This term marks the halfway point of the 70th week of Daniel. Scripture says that the abomination of desolation will occur at this time. The abomination of desolation literally means the abomination that causes desolation, which is when the temple in Jerusalem will be desecrated by the antichrist that is to come (2 Thess. 2:3-4). References to this abomination, of course, point to the midpoint of the 70th week of Daniel, making it easy to place on a timeline and very helpful in understanding the timing of certain events. The midpoint is also called a *time of trouble* (Dan. 12:1), *the time of Jacob's trouble* (Jer. 30:7), *tribulation* (Matt. 24:9), *great tribulation* (Matt. 24:21), and even *the wrath of Satan* (Rev. 12:12). Its timing will fall between the third and fourth seal, which is recorded in the sixth chapter of Revelation. Timelines and charts comparing Scripture with Scripture will be provided throughout this book to assist you in your understanding of prophetic events and the general time associated with them.

Seventy Weeks of Daniel (490 years)

At the time that Daniel received this seventy-week (490 year) prophecy, he and his people (Israel, more specifically Judah) had been in captivity under Babylon for almost seventy years. It was already determined that they would be in captivity for 70 years (Dan. 9:2; Jer. 25:11-12; 29:10). Although no specific sin is recorded of Daniel in Scripture, he prayed, confessing the sins of himself and his people (Dan. 9:4-19). Then Daniel prayed that God would return them to their land. While still praying, the angel Gabriel came to reveal the highpoints of Israel's future and the timeline associated with it. This prophecy revealed the precise time that Israel's awaited Messiah would appear, which, of course, points to Jesus Christ. Anyone who studies this prophecy would know that the Messiah has already come. It is found in Daniel 9:24-27. As we have seen, this is a 490-year period. The prophecy reads as follows:

> 24 *'Seventy weeks are determined upon thy people and upon thy holy city,* to finish the transgression, and to make an end of sins, and to make reconciliation for iniquity, and to bring in everlasting righteousness, and to seal up the

vision and prophecy, and to anoint the most Holy. [25]Know therefore and understand, *that* from the going forth of the commandment to restore and to build Jerusalem unto the Messiah the Prince *shall be* seven weeks, and threescore and two weeks: the street shall be built again, and the wall, even in troublous times. [26]And after threescore and two weeks shall Messiah be cut off, but not for himself: and the people of the prince that shall come shall destroy the city and the sanctuary; and the end thereof *shall be* with a flood, and unto the end of the war desolations are determined. [27]And *he shall confirm the covenant with many for one week:* and in the *midst of the week* he shall cause the sacrifice and the oblation to cease, and for the *overspreading of abominations he shall make it desolate,* even until the consummation, and that determined shall be poured upon the desolate.' (Dan. 9:24-27 KJV, emphasis added)

Verse 24 tells us that seventy weeks (490 years) are literally cut off or out for the nation of Israel and Jerusalem. This time has a purpose (v 24) and the clock would start when a specific decree was given to rebuild the city of Jerusalem, along with its streets and wall (v 25). Although several decrees were given, the one that most completes the guidelines of this decree is found in Nehemiah 2:1-8. King Artaxerxes made this decree in the 20th year of his reign, which was 444 or 445BC. It was made in the Hebrew month of Nisan. History tells us that Artaxerxes began his reign 464BC. Daniel received this prophecy 538 or 539BC (Dan. 9:1). Note that when we count from BC toward AD, the numbers get smaller. This is of course not the case when counting forward in AD, the numbers get larger as each year progresses. From the time that this decree was given (444 or 445BC) would be 483 years until the Messiah (Jesus Christ) would come. It said that there would be *seven weeks* (49 years) and *sixty-two weeks* (434 years) equaling 483 until the Messiah comes (v 25b). This prophecy is divided into three periods of time (7 weeks, 62 weeks, and 1 week.). The first two periods (483 years) have already been fulfilled. At the end of

483 years, the Messiah would be 'cut off' meaning 'killed,' referring to the crucifixion of Jesus Christ (v 26; Matt. 27:32-55; Mark 15:21-41; Luke 23:26-49; John. 19:17-30). At that time, Jesus was rejected as Messiah for the nation of Israel. There is still one 7-year period yet to come that will of course begin at the confirming of a covenant with Israel and the antichrist. The seventy-week prophecy is broken up as follows:

> 7 weeks = 49 years ('to store and build Jerusalem' – Dan. 9:25)
>
> 62 weeks = 434 years ('until Messiah the Prince' – Dan. 9:25)
>
> 1 week = 7 years ('he (antichrist) shall confirm a covenant' – Dan. 9:27)
>
> 70 weeks = 490 years (God would deal with Israel – Dan. 9:24)

British Bible scholar, Sir Robert Anderson, in his book *The Coming Prince*, calculated the first 483-year period of time by converting the 360-day prophecy years into 365 calendar days. The short version goes something like this:

- 360 days x 483 = 173,880 days
- Divide 173,880 days by 365 calendar days and you get 476 years.
  (Artaxerxes decree was made in 444 or 445BC.)
- 476 years minus 445BC = 31 (476 years minus 444BC = 32). Keep in mind that there is no zero BC or AD, so that would make it 32 or 33AD.
- Jesus rode into Jerusalem on the 10th of Nisan in the year 32 or 33AD. He was rejected by the nation of Israel as Messiah and then crucified on the same Passover week on the 14th of Nisan, thereby fulfilling the first 69 weeks (483 years) of this seventy-week (490-year) prophecy.

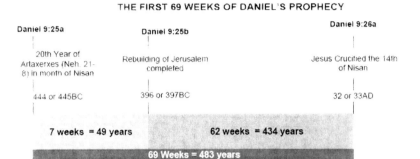

Note: This time line is a breakdown of the first 69 weeks (483 years) of Daniel's seventy-week prophecy, which has already been fulfilled

Seven Years Plus 75 days (30 days plus 45 days)

We have already seen that a 7-year covenant will begin the 70th week of Daniel and at the midpoint the covenant will be broken by the desecration of the Jewish temple. Immediately following this event the persecution of the nation of Israel and those who follow Christ begins. At the end of this 7-year period, Israel will receive Jesus as their Messiah and the nation shall be saved (Dan. 9:24). However, what you may not know is what happens in the 75-day period afterward. It is mentioned in Daniel 12:11-12 and is divided into two sections (a 30 and a 45-day period).

> ¹¹ 'And from the time that the daily sacrifice shall be taken away, and the abomination that maketh desolate set up, there shall be *a thousand two hundred and ninety days.* ¹²Blessed *is* he that waiteth, and cometh to the *thousand three hundred and five and thirty days.* ¹³But go thou thy way till the end *be*: for thou shalt rest, and stand in thy lot at the end of the days.' (Dan. 12:11-13 KJV, emphasis added)

In Hebrew, verse 11 would literally read like this, 'From the time that the daily sacrifice is taken away, to make desolate the abominator, shall be one thousand two hundred and ninety days (1290 days).' In other words, the abominator (antichrist, the beast [Rev. 13:1-10]) will be destroyed 30 days after the 7-year period is over (remember that 1260 days is 3 ½ years, [1260 days + 30 days is 1290 days]). We will see that this period of time is described in the 16th chapter of Revelation, in the seven bowl judgments.

Verse 12 says blessed or happy are those who wait until 1335 days. So, 1260 days + 30 days + 45 days is 1335 days. At this time, the millennial kingdom will begin, when Christ will set-up His earthly rule. Those from the nation of Israel who became believers and survive until the millennial kingdom begins, will enter it without glorified bodies (Is. 65:17-25; Rev. 21:1-4). Therefore, they will continue to live in their natural bodies just as we do today.

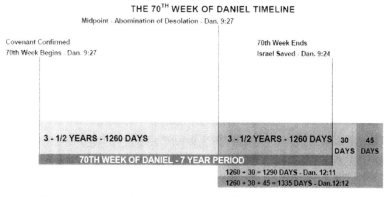

THE 70TH WEEK OF DANIEL TIMELINE
Midpoint - Abomination of Desolation - Dan. 9:27

Covenant Confirmed
70th Week Begins - Dan. 9:27

70th Week Ends
Israel Saved - Dan. 9:24

3 - 1/2 YEARS - 1260 DAYS

3 - 1/2 YEARS - 1260 DAYS   30   45
                          DAYS DAYS

70TH WEEK OF DANIEL - 7 YEAR PERIOD

1260 + 30 = 1290 DAYS - Dan. 12:11
1260 + 30 + 45 = 1335 DAYS - Dan.12:12

Note: This time line is fixed and does not move. By comparing Scripture with Scripture, we will be able to get a basic idea of the timing of certain prophetic events as we build upon this time line throughout this book.

If you already have a basic understanding of Daniel's 70-week prophecy, this chapter was simply a review. However, if it was the first time that you have heard of this prophecy, you may have been somewhat confused at times. That's okay. Take your time and review the material. Get as familiar as possible with the charts. My goal was to get you familiar with Daniel's prophecy, the terminology surrounding it, and the time lines.

Chapter 4

All Wrath is Not the Same

The Day of the Lord – God's Wrath

The purpose of this chapter is to give a clear understanding of the wrath of God (the day of the Lord) and the wrath of Satan (the great tribulation). They are two totally different events that cannot possibly occur at the same time. There is a biblical sign associated with the beginning of each. As a former pre-tribulationist, I unknowingly confused the two events. This caused a misunderstanding about the timing of the rapture. Gaining an understanding of the differences in these events is the main reason I changed my rapture view from a pre-tribulation view to a pre-wrath view. After gaining that understanding, everything else just fell into place.

An understanding of what the day of the LORD *is* and what it *is not*, is an important key to having an accurate understanding of what will happen in the end times. Differences in rapture views literally come from what one understands about the day of the LORD (God's wrath). Keep in mind that the day of the LORD is not a 24-hour day. It is a period of time that will be determined by God. Of course, the best place to find out about this time period is

Scripture. There is a tremendous amount of information in the Bible written about the day of the LORD. I will give you just a few of them. As you read each passage, pay attention to whom God directs his wrath, who is exalted, how the inhabitants of the earth react, and the cosmic signs in the heavens (moon, stars, and sun). These will be key points as we study together.

[9]'Behold, the *day of the LORD* cometh, *cruel both with wrath and fierce anger, to lay the land desolate: and he shall destroy the sinners thereof out of it.* [10]For the stars of heaven and the constellations thereof shall not give their light: *the sun shall be darkened in his going forth, and the moon shall not cause her light to shine.* [11]*And I will punish the world for their evil, and the wicked for their iniquity;* and I will cause the arrogancy of the proud to cease, and will lay low the haughtiness of the terrible.'..... [13]'Therefore I will shake the heavens, and the earth shall remove out of her place, in the *wrath of the LORD* of hosts, and in the day of his fierce anger.' (Is. 13:9-11, 13 KJV, emphasis added)

[15]'Alas for the day! For *the day of the LORD is at hand, and as a destruction from the Almighty shall it come.*' (Joel 1:15 KJV, emphasis added)

[1]'Blow ye the trumpet in Zion, and sound an alarm in my holy mountain: let all the *inhabitants of the land tremble:* for *the day of the LORD* cometh, for *it is* nigh at hand; [2]*A day of darkness and of gloominess, a day of clouds and of thick darkness,* as the morning spread upon the mountains.' (Joel 2:1-2a KJV, emphasis added)

[10]'The earth shall quake before them; *the heavens shall tremble: the sun and the moon shall be dark, and the stars shall withdraw their shining:* [11]And the LORD shall utter his voice before his army: for his camp *is* very great: for *he is* strong that executeth his word: *for the day of.the LORD*

is great and very terrible; and who can abide it?' (Joel 2:10-11 KJV, emphasis added)

[18] 'Woe unto you that desire the *day of the LORD! to* what end *is* it for you? *the day of the LORD is darkness, and not light.* [19]As if a man did flee from a lion, and a bear met him; or went into the house, and leaned his hand on the wall, and a serpent bit him. [20]*Shall not the day of the LORD be darkness, and not light? even very dark, and no brightness in it?'* (Amos 5:18-20 KJV, emphasis added)

[14] *'The great day of the LORD is near, it is near, and* hasteth greatly, even the voice of *the day of the LORD: the* [15]*mighty man shall cry there bitterly.* [15]*That day is a day of wrath, a day of trouble and distress, a day of wasteness and desolation, a day of darkness and gloominess, a day of clouds and thick darkness,* [16]*A day of the trumpet and alarm* against the fenced cities, and against the high towers.' (Zeph. 1:14-16 KJV, emphasis added)

[7] 'But the heavens and the earth, which are now, by the same word are kept in store, *reserved unto fire against the day of judgment and perdition of ungodly men.'* [10] 'But the day of the Lord will come as a thief in the night; in the which the heavens shall pass away with a great noise, and the elements shall melt with fervent heat, the earth also and the works that are therein shall be burned up.' (2 Pet. 3:7, 10 KJV, emphasis added)

[16] 'And said to the mountains and rocks, 'Fall on us, and hide us from the face of him that sitteth on the throne, and from *the wrath of the Lamb:* [17]*For the great day of his wrath is come; and who shall be able to stand?''* (Rev. 6:16-17 KJV, emphasis added)

[9] 'The Lord knoweth how to deliver the godly out of temptations, *and to reserve the unjust unto the day of*

judgment to be punished.' (2 Pet. 2:9 KJV, emphasis added)

[30] 'And I will show wonders in the heavens and in the earth, blood, and fire, and pillars of smoke. [31]*The sun shall be turned into darkness, and the moon into blood, before* the *great and the terrible day of the LORD come.'* (Joel 2:30-31 KJV, emphasis added)

As we can see, Scripture reveals that the day of the LORD will be a time of God's wrath, anger, and fury. It will be a terrible time when His wrath will be poured out on this wicked world. The wicked sinners will be punished for their wicked deeds. The arrogant and proud will be brought low. It will be a time of destruction and gloom for the ungodly. It will be a time of earthquakes. The heavens will shake and no one will escape. It will also be a time of divine darkness (cosmic disturbances). The moon and the sun will be divinely darkened *before* the day of the Lord begins. The inhabitants of the earth will tremble with fear.

Isaiah said that during this day, 'The lofty looks of man shall be humbled, the haughtiness of men shall be bowed down, and the *LORD alone shall be exalted in that day. For the day of the LORD of hosts shall come upon everything proud and lofty, upon everything lifted up and it shall be brought low...* the loftiness of man shall be bowed down, and the haughtiness of men shall be brought low; *the LORD alone will be exalted in that day'* (Is. 2:11-12, 17 NKJV, emphasis added). Notice that only the LORD will be exalted in that day, no one else, only God. All who exalt themselves and all who are proud and lifted up will be brought low and judged (punished) by God. This would mean that the day of the LORD will not be a time when the antichrist or Satan will rule the earth.

Although the day of the LORD is a time of judgment on the wicked, it is also a time of deliverance and salvation of the righteous (2 Pet. 2:9). I hope you noticed that the day of the LORD is not a time experienced by God's saints and those who keep God's commandments and hold the testimony of Jesus Christ.

Those in Christ are not appointed unto God's wrath (Rom. 5:9; 1 Thess. 5:9). Paul said in 1 Thessalonians 1:9-10 NKJV, 'For they themselves declare concerning us what manner of entry we had to you, and how you turned to God from idols to serve the living and true God, and to wait for His Son from heaven, whom He raised from the dead, *even* Jesus who *delivers us from the wrath to come.*' This is an important point to remember. So, keep this in mind, the godly will *not* have to endure the day of the LORD (God's wrath). Make a mental note. If you see the godly being persecuted as you will see in the Olivet Discourse (Matt. 24:9-12; Mark 13:9,12-13), and Rev. 6:9-11; 12:17; and 13:7, it *cannot*, I will repeat, it *cannot* be God's wrath (the day of the Lord).

We just looked at God's wrath. What did we find out about it? I will list some of our findings below. They will be compared with what Scripture says about Satan's wrath (the great tribulation).

Concerning the day of the LORD:

- Only the LORD is exalted in that day. (Is. 2:11, 17)
- Only the wicked will be punished. (Is.13:11)
- It is a day of judgment for the ungodly. (2 Pet. 3:7)
- It is accompanied by darkness 'cosmic disturbances.' (Joel 2:10-11; Zeph. 1:15)
- Cosmic disturbances come *before* God's wrath begins. (Joel 2:30-31)
- It is a day of trumpet alarms. (Joel 2:1; Zeph. 1:16)
- The godly will be delivered / rescued. (2 Pet. 2:9)
- Inhabitants of the earth will tremble. (Joel 2:1)

Satan's Wrath – The Great Tribulation

Since we have looked at God's wrath, let us now take a look at what the Scriptures say about Satan's wrath (the great tribulation) and compare it with what we have learned about God's wrath (the day of the LORD). Are the two happening at the same time or is it impossible according to Scripture? Many will say that they are happening at the same time; however, you will plainly see that according to Scripture, it is impossible for the two to occur at the same time. As you read the following Scriptures, pay attention to who is being persecuted (the righteous or the unrighteous) and who is doing the persecuting. Is it God or Satan? Who is being exalted during this time? Is it God or Satan?

[21] "For then shall be *great tribulation,* such as was not since the beginning of the world to this time, no, nor ever shall be. [22]*And except those days should be shortened, there should no flesh be saved: but for the elect's sake those days shall be shortened."* (Matt. 24:21-22 KJV, emphasis added)

[12] "Therefore rejoice, *ye* heavens, and ye that dwell in them. Woe to the inhabiters of the earth and of the sea! for the *devil is come down unto you, having great wrath, because he knoweth that he hath but a short time."* (Rev.12:12 KJV, emphasis added)

[17] "And the dragon (Satan) was wroth with the woman (Israel), and *went to make war with the remnant of her seed, which keep the commandments of God, and have the testimony of Jesus Christ."* (Rev.12:17 KJV, emphasis added)

*Note: It is clear in Scripture that the dragon is Satan (Rev. 12:9). However, the reason that the woman is listed as Israel is because of the description in Revelation 12:1-6, Joseph's dream in Genesis 37:9-11, and elsewhere in Scripture.

[4] "And they worshipped the dragon which gave power unto the beast (antichrist): and *they worshipped the beast,* saying, 'Who *is* like unto the beast? Who is able to make war with him?' " (Rev. 13:4 KJV, emphasis added)

[3] "Let no man deceive you by any means: for *that day shall not come*, except there come a falling away first, and *that man of sin be revealed, the son of perdition.* [4]*Who opposeth and exalteth himself above all that is called God, or that is worshipped; so that he as God sitteth in the temple of God, showing himself that he is God.*" (2 Thess. 2:3-4 KJV, emphasis added)

[7] "And it was *given unto him* (the antichrist) *to make war with the saints, and to overcome them: and power was given him* over all kindreds, and tongues, and nations. [8]*And all that dwell upon the earth shall worship him, whose names are not written in the book of life of the Lamb slain from the foundation of the world.*" (Rev. 13:7-8 KJV, emphasis added)

We see that Satan will make war against the saints of God (the faithful believers of Jesus Christ who do not deny His name). The antichrist will exalt himself above God and demand worship. This time of great tribulation will be shortened for the sake of the elect. Only the lost will worship the antichrist and Satan. It is quite easy to see that God's wrath (the day of the LORD) and the wrath of Satan are not the same event. During the day of the Lord, God punishes the ungodly and during the great tribulation (Satan's wrath), Satan persecutes the godly. So, these two events must be separated to begin to properly understand these events. It should also be noted that Satan's wrath will be cut short for the sake of the elect. If it were not, they (the elect) would not survive the persecution of the antichrist.

Concerning Satan's wrath:

- The antichrist will exalt himself and demand worship. (2 Thess. 2:4)
- Only the godly, the saints, and the faithful believers

will be persecuted. (Rev. 12:17)

- Cosmic disturbances are *not* linked to this time.

God's Wrath (the day of the Lord) vs. Satan's Wrath (the great tribulation)

Let us review what we have seen that Scripture reveals about God's wrath and Satan's wrath. Understanding these differences is foundational for a proper biblical view of the end times and the rapture.

There is great confusion about God's wrath and Satan's wrath in the last days. Although many very good Bible teachers confuse the two, a comparison will show that they are two different events. Let us begin this comparison: Isaiah 2:17 NKJV (in context of the day of the Lord) says, 'The loftiness of man shall be bowed down, and the haughtiness of men shall be brought low; *The LORD alone will be exalted in that day.*' Yet in 2 Thessalonians 2:3-4 NKJV, Paul writes speaking of the antichrist, 'Let no one deceive you by any means; for that Day *(the day of the LORD)* will not come unless the falling away comes first, and the man of sin is revealed, the son of perdition, *who opposes and exalts himself above all that is called God or that is worshiped*, so that he sits as God in the temple of God, showing himself that he is God.' Okay, we see that only the LORD will be exalted during the day of the LORD. This is a direct contrast with the great tribulation period. During which, the antichrist will exalt himself. Paul (in 2 Thess. 2:2-3) confirms what Daniel said. Daniel 11:36 NKJV says, 'Then the king (the antichrist) shall do according to his own will: *he shall exalt and magnify himself above every god*, shall speak blasphemies against the God of gods, and shall prosper till the wrath has been accomplished; for what has been determined shall be done.' If these two events (the wrath of God and the wrath of Satan) are not separated, we have a great contradiction in Scripture. This cannot be. Obviously, they are two separate events.

In Revelation 12:12, the devil comes down with *great wrath*. In verse 17, the dragon *makes war against those that keep the*

commandments of God and have the testimony of Jesus Christ.
Revelation 13:7 says that the antichrist is granted power to make
war with the saints and to overcome them. Obviously, only the
righteous on earth will be persecuted during Satan's wrath. Why
would the antichrist persecute the unrighteous (wicked)? They are
following him. So, his wrath is poured out on the righteous (who
refuse to follow him and receive his mark). Yet during God's
wrath, Peter says in 2 Peter 2:9 NKJV, 'The Lord knows how to
deliver the godly out of temptations (testing) and to reserve the
unjust under punishment for the day of judgment.' If the godly are
rescued and the unjust are reserved punishment for the Day of
Judgment; how can they occur at the same time? 2 Peter 3:7 NKJV
says, 'But the heavens and the earth which are now preserved by
the same word, are *reserved for fire until the day of judgment and
perdition of ungodly men.*' So we also see that only the true
followers of Christ (the saints, the godly, the one's who keep the
commandments of God and have the testimony of Jesus Christ) are
persecuted during the wrath of Satan (the great tribulation) and the
wrath of God is reserved for the unjust. Again, showing that the
two events cannot be the same. Since this is the case, then in the
context of the end times, whenever you find the godly, the elect,
the saints, or those who keep the commandments of Jesus Christ
being persecuted, they are not being persecuted by God, and it is
not God's wrath. They are being persecuted by Satan and are under
Satan's wrath. Satan's wrath is obviously the great tribulation.
Clearly, the wrath of God upon the unjust follows the persecution
of believers.

If the study of the end times (eschatology) is new to you, you
might say, 'What's the big deal?' Well, it is a big deal. I will
explain. The pre-tribulation view argues that they are the same
event. A pre-tribulationist must say this to be able to make the
rapture imminent (by their definition of imminent, *they* mean that
it [the rapture] can occur at any moment, without a sign). They also
want to keep the church out of the tribulation/great tribulation
period to come. Why? They teach and believe that the church will
not experience this time of trouble and will be removed from the

earth before any persecution from the antichrist. They have a flawed understanding of what the tribulation or great tribulation is. In the pre-tribulation view circle, it is thought and taught that the great tribulation is God's wrath. When one begins with that flawed understanding, they will err on the timing of the rapture and other end-time events. If the two events (God's wrath and Satan's wrath) are different (which they are), this means that the church will be here on earth to experience the wrath of the antichrist.

By taking Scripture at face value in our comparison, we see that during Satan's wrath (the great tribulation when the antichrist is given power), he exalts himself and blasphemies God. During this time, the saints (the godly) are persecuted. The very opposite happens during the day of the LORD (God's wrath). Only the LORD is exalted during that time. The godly are rescued and the ungodly will receive judgment. We have now seen that Scripture clearly teaches that these are two separate events that *cannot* possibly be happening at the same time.

The Great Tribulation

Now that we have gotten a clear understanding about the differences in God's wrath (the day of the Lord) and Satan's wrath (the great tribulation), it is probably a good idea to see what the Scriptures specifically say about the great tribulation. The words *great tribulation* are used only three times in the Bible. It comes from two Greek words, *thlipsis* (Strong's # 2347) meaning *pressure*, *persecution* or *trouble* and *megas* (Strong's # 3173) meaning *large, strong, or great*. The words are used twice by Jesus and once by John to describe what he saw during the revelation that Jesus gave him. What is the great tribulation? Who will experience it? To find this out, we will look at what Scripture says. Each is in context of the end times.

Let us first look at the 24th chapter of Matthew (the Olivet Discourse). Some say that since Matthew is the Jewish gospel, it is not referring to the church. Scholars have reason to believe that Matthew's main intended audience was the Jews. Yet, out of all four gospels, Matthew is the only gospel that mentions the church by name (Matt. 16:18 once and 18:17 twice). It mentions the church three times. Matthew's gospel ends with the Great Commission (Matt. 28:16-20), which almost everyone agrees is addressing the church. In Mark's gospel, the Gentiles (non-Jews) are the predominate audience. However, it contains the Olivet Discourse in the 13th chapter also. Having said that, let us look at the biblical passages that mention the great tribulation.

> [21] 'For then shall be *great tribulation*, such as was not since the beginning of the world to this time, no, nor ever shall be. [22]And except those days should be shortened, there should no flesh be saved: but for the elect's sake those days shall be shortened.' (Matt. 24:21-22 KJV, emphasis added)

In Matthew 24, it is clear that this *great tribulation refers to the persecution of the elect.* We can also see that this time of great tribulation will be shortened for the elect's sake. The 13th chapter of Mark, the parallel chapter to Matthew 24, it simply is called *tribulation* (Mark 13:19). In other words, the word *tribulation* and *great tribulation* are referring to the same event (the second half of the 70th week of Daniel).

The second appearance of the *great tribulation* is found in Revelation 2. The book of Revelation is addressed to the bondservants of Christ (Rev. 1:1). The mention of *great tribulation* is found in Revelation 2:22.

> [21] 'And I gave her space to repent of her fornication; and she repented not. [22]Behold, I will cast her into a bed, and them that commit adultery with her into *great tribulation,* except they repent of their deeds. [23]And I will kill her children with death; and all the churches shall know that I am he which searcheth the reins and hearts: and I will give unto every one of you according to your works.' (Rev. 2:21-23 KJV, emphasis added)

Clearly Jesus is addressing the church of Thyatira. Because some of them where unfaithful, they (the unfaithful ones) will be cast into *great tribulation*. I am *not* saying that this is *the great tribulation* that Jesus spoke of in Matthew 24:21. Nevertheless, it is tribulation. Through this, *the minds and hearts of those in this great tribulation will be searched.* Did not David say, 'Search me, O God, and know my heart: try me, and know my thoughts: And see if there be any wicked way in me, and lead me in the way everlasting' (Psalm 139:23-24 KJV). Jesus told Peter, 'Simon, Simon, behold, Satan hath desired to have you (plural in Greek), that he may sift you as wheat: But I have prayed for thee (singular in Greek), that thy faith fail not: and when thou art converted, strengthen thy brethren' (Luke 22:31-32 KJV). Testing only purifies a true believer and shows what he or she really is, all the while drawing that person closer to the Lord.

The third and final time that we find the great tribulation mentioned is in Revelation 7. It is during a scene in heaven with a great multitude, which no one could number. The timeline of this event is between the breaking of the 6th and 7th seal. This occurs *after* the antichrist is revealed (Rev. 6:1-2, first seal), *after* the persecution and martyrdom of many believers (Rev. 6:9-11, fifth seal), and *after* cosmic disturbances (the darkening of the sun, moon, and stars, Rev. 6:12-16, sixth seal). These cosmic disturbances come *before* the day of the Lord/God's wrath (Joel 2:1, 2a; Acts 2:20).

> ^{9} 'After this I beheld, and, lo, a great multitude, which no man could number, of all nations, and kindreds, and people, and tongues, *stood* before the throne, and before the Lamb, clothed with white robes, and *palms in their hand;*' ^{14} 'And I said unto him, 'Sir, thou knowest.' And he said to me, 'These are they which came *out of great tribulation*, and have washed their robes, and made them white in the blood of the Lamb.'' (Rev. 7:9, 14 KJV, emphasis added)

Not only is the timing of this appearance of the great multitude in heaven remarkable, but also how they are described. They are described as *standing* before the throne (not as souls under the altar as in Rev. 6:9) and holding palm branches in their hands. It appears that they have their glorified bodies. The believers' glorified bodies will only be received after the rapture occurs (1 Cor. 15:50-53), which occurs at the coming (*parousia*) of the Lord Jesus (1 Thess. 4:15-17) when the dead in Christ and those who are alive and survive are caught up with Christ. Notice that this great multitude standing before the throne has come out of the great tribulation. It is obvious that the souls under the altar (at the 5th seal, Rev. 6:9-11) came out of the great tribulation also, but they are not described in the same manner as the great multitude.

What does all this mean? Scripture says that the elect will go into the great tribulation (Matt. 24:21-22). Scripture also says that this *great multitude will come out of the great tribulation*, thereby identifying the *elect* with the *great multitude*. Another thing that we saw is that the great tribulation will be cut short for the sake of the elect (Matt. 24:22). Because of the severity of the persecution, the elect would not survive if it were not cut short. Now think about that, God will punish the wicked and rescue the godly (2 Thess. 2:6-7; 2 Pet. 2:9). The wicked will be punished during the day of the Lord. Keep in mind that the day of the Lord does not come until after cosmic disturbances (darkening of the sun, moon, and stars) (Joel 2:31; Acts 2:20). In the book of Revelation, we do not find cosmic disturbances until the 6th seal (Rev. 6:12-14). Since believers are not appointed to God's wrath (1 Thess. 5:9; Rom. 5:9), it would make sense that the rapture would occur precisely where we find the great multitude appear in heaven (Rev. 7:9-15). Comparing the appearance of the great multitude in heaven with the elect in the Olivet Discourse, it is easy to see that they are the same event (Matt. 24:29-31; Mark 13:24-27; Luke 21:25-28, where we see the elect gathered together). See the chapter 6 for more detail.

Review

Satan's Wrath

- The antichrist will exalt himself and demand worship.

(2 Thess. 2:4)
- Only the godly, the saints, faithful believers will be persecuted. (Rev. 12:17)
- Cosmic Disturbances are *not* linked to this time.

God's Wrath

- Only the LORD is exalted in that day. (Is. 2:11, 17)
- Only the wicked will be punished. (Is.13:11)
- A day of judgment for the ungodly. (2 Pet. 3:7)
- It is accompanied by darkness 'cosmic disturbances.' (Joel 2:10-11; Zeph. 1:15)
- Cosmic disturbances come *before* God's wrath begins. (Joel 2:30-31)
- A day of trumpet alarms. (Joel 2:1; Zeph. 1:16)
- The godly will be delivered / rescued. (2 Pet. 2:9)
- The inhabitants of the earth will tremble. (Joel 2:1)

Chapter 5

The Parousia (Coming) of Christ

In this chapter, we will discover what the *coming* of Christ actually means. We will see what events are associated with it and how they are tied together. Understanding this holds a vital piece to the rapture puzzle. There are several Greek words that are translated as 'coming' in the New Testament. However, we will take a look at only two of them, and our main focus will be on one. The first word is *erchomai* (Strong's #2064); it is a verb, which means *to come or to go*. An example would be, 'He is *coming* down the street.' It means specifically *coming* from one place to another.

The other word for *coming* is *parousia* (Strong's #3952); it is a noun, which means *a presence* or *presence with*. It comes from two Greek words that literally mean *being with* (*para*, 'with,' and *ousia* 'being'). It is an event. This word is used to describe Jesus' second coming (*parousia*) in its entirety. This means not just His arrival (glorious appearing [Titus 2:13]), but also His continual presence from beginning to end. The glorious appearing of Christ refers to His initial *coming in glory at the rapture*. In general, the 2nd 'coming' (*parousia*) of Christ will include the resurrection of those dead in Christ, the rapture of believers, and the wrath of God upon the unrighteous who remain on earth (the day of the Lord).

After this He will set up His earthly kingdom. In the King James Version, the word '*parousia*' is translated as *coming* twenty-two times, eighteen of these times it is used prophetically (seventeen times for the coming of Jesus and one time for the coming of the antichrist). It is twice translated as 'presence' (2 Cor. 10:10; Phil. 2:12), which of course is in contrast to absence.

In *Vine's Expository Dictionary of Old and New Testament Words,* W.E. Vine said concerning the word *parousia,* '...denotes both an 'arrival' and a consequent 'presence with.' For instance, in a papyrus letter a lady speaks of the necessity of her *parousia* in a place in order to attend to matters relating to her property there.' [1]

Many events occurred during Jesus' first coming (*parousia*). Of course, Jesus was born, but it is *not* limited to just that one aspect. His first coming (*parousia*) included His actual birth, later at the age of twelve in the temple, being baptized by John the Baptist, beginning His earthly ministry, performing many miracles, instituting the Lord's Supper, to His crucifixion, death and burial, His resurrection from the dead and later ascension into heaven. All these events occurred at His first coming (*parousia*) and are viewed as only one coming (*parousia*), not several. It was His first continual presence with us. However, during His first coming (*parousia*), He would come and go (*erchomai*) many places.

The word *parousia* is also used when referring to the coming (*parousia*) of the antichrist, who will be empowered by Satan. 2 Thessalonians 2:9 NKJV says, 'The *coming* of the lawless one (the antichrist) is according to the working of Satan, with all power, signs, and lying wonders' (emphasis added). The coming (*parousia*) here refers to the continual presence of the antichrist. This includes his rise to power and the performance of signs and his lying (false) wonders. His coming (*parousia*) will also include his persecution of all those who trust in Jesus Christ (Rev. 12:17; 13:7).

Different Emphasis

Jesus referred to His second coming (*parousia*) while sitting on the Mount of Olives. The disciples asked Jesus, in Matthew 24:3b

NKJV, 'Tell us, when will these things be? And what will be the sign of Your *coming* (*parousia*), and of the end of the age?' We saw that *parousia* literally means *being with*. In Scripture, you will see a subtle emphasis on different aspects of His coming (*parousia*). The use of the word *coming* (*parousia*) sometimes emphasizes the rapture and resurrection of believers at the beginning (glorious appearing) of Christ's coming (1 Cor. 15:23; 1 Thess. 4:15; 1 Thess. 5:23; 2 Thess. 2:1; James 5:7-8; 2 Pet. 3:4; 1 John 2:28), and other times it emphasizes the day of the Lord, when God's wrath is poured out on the wicked (Matt. 24:37, 39; 2 Thess. 2:8; 2 Pet. 3:12). Yet, no matter the emphasis, they all speak of His second coming (one continual presence), not a 2nd and then a 3rd coming. This means not a rapture and a separate second coming, but the rapture and the second coming are the same event. The rapture occurs at the second coming.

It is commonly said in the pre-tribulational view that the rapture is not the second coming of Christ. They say that at the rapture, Christ comes for the church, but at His second coming, seven years later, He comes with His church. It is declared that there are two separate events. Even educated Bible teachers who hold the pre-tribulation view will say this. A professor in a systematic theology class I took even said this. It is what I initially learned. However, this is not what the Bible says. Keep in mind that this is a continual presence. Once it begins, it continues. Let us allow Scripture to interpret Scripture.

Emphasis on the Rapture and/or Resurrection at Christ's Coming (Parousia)

[23] 'But every man in his own order: Christ the firstfruits; afterward they that are Christ's at his *coming*.' (1 Cor. 15:23 KJV, emphasis added)

[15] 'For this we say unto you by the word of the Lord, that we which are alive and remain unto the *coming* of the Lord shall not prevent them which are asleep.' (1 Thess.

4:15 KJV, emphasis added)

[23] 'And the very God of peace sanctify you wholly; and I pray God your whole spirit and soul and body be preserved blameless unto the *coming* of our Lord Jesus Christ.' (1 Thess. 5:23 KJV, emphasis added)

[1] 'Now we beseech you, brethren, by the *coming* of our Lord Jesus Christ, and by our gathering together unto him.' (2 Thess. 2:1 KJV, emphasis added)

[7] 'Be patient therefore, brethren, unto the *coming* of the Lord. Behold, the husbandman waiteth for the precious fruit of the earth, and hath long patience for it, until he receive the early and latter rain. [8]Be ye also patient; stablish your hearts: for the *coming* of the Lord draweth nigh.' (James 5:7-8 KJV, emphasis added)

[4] 'And saying, Where is the promise of his *coming*? for since the fathers fell asleep, all things continue as they were from the beginning of the creation.' (2 Pet. 3:4 KJV, emphasis added)

[28] 'And now, little children, abide in him; that, when he shall appear, we may have confidence, and not be ashamed before him at his *coming*.' (1 John 2:28 KJV, emphasis added)

What have we seen emphasized in the previous verses concerning Christ's second coming (*parousia*)?

1. The resurrection occurs at Christ's second coming (1 Cor. 15:23).
2. The church will remain on earth and not be raptured until Christ's second coming (1 Thess. 4:15).
3. Christ's second coming and our gathering together (rapture) are closely related and in fact are the same

event (2 Thess. 2:1).

4. Christ appears at His second coming (1 John 2:28).

Christ's second coming initiates the day of the Lord (God's wrath). Scripture says the day of the Lord is preceded by cosmic disturbances (signs in the sun, moon, and stars). Since Christ's second coming is associated with this and the rapture occurs at the same time, it is not possible for the rapture be a signless event. There will be a harvest at the end of the age (Matt. 13:24-30, 37-43, 47-50) where Jesus will send His angels to separate the wicked and righteous. There are two things that occur at Christ's second coming, the rapture and the day of the Lord. As in the days of Noah, these events will occur on the same day. The righteous will be rescued (raptured) and the wicked will be judged (God's judgment of the wicked will begin on earth). If this is the case, there cannot be a seven-year separation between the rapture and wrath of God. Also, there cannot be a seven-year separation between the rapture and Christ's second coming. If you take these previous verses at face value, you can see that Christ's second coming (*parousia*) and the rapture are *not* two separate events, but indeed are the same. If this is what Scripture says (and it does), how can the rapture and the second coming of Christ be separated? The pre-tribulationist argues that these events are separate, even years apart. Scripture says otherwise. For the pre-tribulation view to be accurate, technically there would have to be a 2nd and 3rd coming of Christ. And we know this is not the case.

Emphasis on the Day of the Lord (God's wrath) at Christ's Coming (Parousia)

[37] 'But as the days of Noe (Noah) *were*, so shall also the *coming* of the Son of man be.' (Matt. 24:37 KJV, emphasis added)

[39] 'And knew not until the flood came, and took them all away; so shall also the *coming* of the Son of man be.'

(Matt. 24:39 KJV, emphasis added)

[8] 'And then shall that Wicked be revealed, whom the Lord shall consume with the spirit of his mouth, and shall destroy with the brightness of his *coming*.' (2 Thess. 2:8 KJV, emphasis added)

[12] 'Looking for and hasting unto the *coming* of the day of God, wherein the heavens being on fire shall be dissolved, and the elements shall melt with fervent heat.' (2 Pet. 3:12 KJV, emphasis added)

What have we seen emphasized in the previous verses concerning Christ's second coming (*parousia*)?

1. Christ's second coming will be like the days of Noah (Matt. 24:37, 39). The righteous will be rescued and the wicked will be punished and/or destroyed. It is interesting to note that the two events happened on the same day.
2. The lawless one (the antichrist) will be destroyed (*katargeo* [Strongs #2673], *reduced to inactivity*) at Christ's second coming (2 Thess. 2:8).

At Christ's second coming (*parousia*), He will rescue the righteous and destroy the wicked. The antichrist's power or rule will be brought to nothing (2 Thess. 2:8). Why? This is so because only God will be exalted in the day of the Lord (Is. 2:11, 17). If the antichrist's rule will be brought to nothing at Christ's *coming* and the rapture occurs at Christ's *coming*, how could it be possible for the rapture to occur *before* the 70th week of Daniel (also referred to as the tribulation period) begins. The antichrist comes on the scene at the *beginning* of this seven-year block of time and does not begin his worldwide persecution of the elect until the midpoint. So it has to be clear that Christ's second coming does not occur until after the midpoint of the tribulation (70th week of Daniel).

44

Putting It All Together

In Scripture, we have seen that there are subtle differences in the use of the word *coming* (*parousia*). Since there will be only one second coming (*parousia*) of Christ, several things will be tied together.

Christ will appear at His second coming (1 John 2:28). The church will remain on earth until Christ's second coming. At the second coming, there will be the resurrection of all who are in Christ (1 Cor. 15:23; 1 Thess. 4:15), the gathering together (rapture) of the elect, saints, or church will occur at this time (2 Thess. 2:1). This time will be like in the days of Noah (Matt. 24:37, 39) when the righteous were rescued and the wicked were destroyed. The antichrist will be in power on earth; however, his rule will be rendered useless at the coming of Christ (2 Thess. 2:8). This will be a time of fiery judgment on earth (2 Pet. 3:12).

2 Thessalonians 1:3-10 supports the above thought in Scripture. The saints will be persecuted and endure tribulation from the wicked (v 4), but when Jesus is revealed from heaven (v 7) at His coming, He will repay with tribulation those who troubled the saints. He will take vengeance on those who do not know God (v 8), and give rest to those who are troubled [the persecuted saints] (v 7). For more detail, read the chapter on Thessalonians.

What must occur 'before' the Coming (parousia) of Christ?

There are several things that must occur *before* the coming (*parousia*) of Christ, day of the Lord, and the gathering together (rapture) of the saints (2 Thess. 2:1-3). Some of these things are found in 2 Thessalonians 2:1-12. More detail about them can also be found in the chapter on Thessalonians.

1. Man of Sin, son of perdition (the antichrist) is revealed, (v 3)
2. Apostasy, (v 3)
3. The antichrist exalts himself, sits as God, and demands

worship, (v 4)

4. He who restrains is taken out of the way, (v 7)
5. Great signs and lying wonders are performed by the antichrist, (v 9)
6. A strong delusion from God will be sent, so all who take pleasure in unrighteous will be condemned, (v 11)

*Christ's second coming will occur only *after* the above events. His coming includes the resurrection and gathering together (the rapture, 1 Thess. 4:15-17). If all of these things must occur *before* the coming of Christ, then how can the rapture occur before the 70th week of Daniel or beginning of the great tribulation? Quite simply, it cannot.

Chapter 6

Matthew 24 – The Olivet Discourse

The 24th chapter of Matthew is traditionally called the Olivet Discourse, because the conversation took place on the Mount of Olives just east of the temple across the Kidron Valley. This conversation took place privately between the disciples and Jesus in approximately 30 to 33 A.D. on the Tuesday evening of the very week that Jesus was crucified. The temple was still under construction and had been since 20 B.C. It would not be completed until 64 A.D., yet, would be destroyed in 70 A.D., which Jesus predicted (Matt. 24:1-2). Now, the prediction was for the temple itself, not the temple mount which stands today. Its destruction would be so complete that not one stone of the temple would be left upon another. Jesus' prediction of the temple destruction is what sparked the questions to follow.

The Olivet Discourse (Matt. 24:3-51 and chapter 25; Mark 13:3-37) is the most critical passage concerning the timing of the coming of Christ, the end of the age, the rapture, and God's wrath, which immediately follows. It is the single most important prophetic text outside the book of Revelation. Specific signs are given that are associated with Christ's coming and the rapture of the elect. Jesus makes reference to Daniel's prophecy concerning the abomination of desolation (Matt. 24:15; Dan. 9:27) and the persecution of the elect by the antichrist. On the whole, the *overview* of the end times is found in the Olivet Discourse, the *time line* is found in Daniel and the *detail* is found Revelation. Each should be compared with one another. By comparing Scripture with Scripture, you will get a full picture of the end-time events and a solid understanding. Although most of the detail is found in Revelation, enough details are given in Matthew and Daniel to place them on a timeline.

Many teach that the church will not be on the earth during the events described in the Olivet Discourse. Those who hold the pre-tribulation view usually say that Jesus is speaking to the nation of Israel only because of the references to Judea and the Sabbath. They therefore, have to make the timing of the events in the Olivet Discourse after the events describing the rapture in 1 Thessalonians 4:13-17, because if they did not, it would disprove to pre-tribulation view. This is an attempt to make the rapture of the church 'imminent,' by imminent, meaning it (the rapture) could happen at any time without a sign. In the pre-tribulation view, the rapture and the return of Christ are separated, making them two separate events that occur years apart. If the church is on earth during the Olivet Discourse, then the timing of the rapture, taught by those who hold the pre-tribulation view cannot be correct. Although it may be widely taught, the teaching of a signless return of Christ is not biblical. Comparing Scripture with Scripture will prove this. Previously in chapter 5 ('The Parousia [Coming] of Christ'), we learned that the rapture occurs at the second coming of Christ.

Who does the Olivet Discourse Apply to?

Some time ago, I asked a pre-tribulation professor to read this chapter. His only comment was that the book of Matthew was a Jewish gospel and the Olivet Discourse did not apply to the church. He really did not appear to want to discuss the matter any further. You see, if the church is on earth during the events described in the

Olivet Discourse, the pre-tribulation rapture view is wrong. Yet, if our desire is to be truly biblically accurate, we must answer this one question, 'Who does the Olivet Discourse apply to? Israel, the church, or does it apply to both?' Let us review. To begin, I will point out that Matthew is the only gospel that mentions the church by name (Matt. 16:18 and 18:17).

The Church is Prophesied

[18] 'And I say also unto thee, That thou art Peter, and upon this rock I will build my *church*; and the gates of hell shall not prevail against it.' (Matt. 16:18 KJV, emphasis added)

The Church is Instructed

[17] 'And if he shall neglect to hear them, tell *it* unto the *church*: but if he neglect to hear the *church,* let him be unto thee as an heathen man and a publican.' (Matt. 18:17 KJV, emphasis added)

The Great Commission

[18] 'And Jesus came and spake unto them, saying, All power is given unto me in heaven and in earth. [19]Go ye therefore, and teach all nations, baptizing them in the name of the Father, and of the Son, and of the Holy Ghost: [20]Teaching them to observe all things whatsoever I have commanded you: and, lo, I am with you alway, *even* unto the end of the world (age).' (Matt. 28:18-20 KJV)

There is no doubt that the Great Commission applies to the church. If the church is prophesied, instructed, and commissioned in Matthew's gospel, why would the Olivet Discourse not apply to the church? We must all at least agree that some portions of Matthew's gospel apply to the church. The Olivet Discourse is also recorded in the 13th chapter of Mark's gospel (a gospel most experts call the Gentile gospel). Some of the points of the Olivet Discourse are also addressed in the 21st chapter of the Luke's gospel. Matthew 24:4-8, Mark 13:4-6, and Luke 21:7-8 are all very similar verses. Jesus gives the same warning, not to be deceived when looking for Christ's return.

[4] 'Tell us, when shall these things be? and what shall be the sign when all these things shall be fulfilled? [5]And Jesus answering them began to say, *Take heed lest any man deceive you:* [6]*For many shall come in my name, saying, 'I am Christ;' and shall deceive many.'* (Mark 13:4-6 KJV, emphasis added)

[8] 'And he said, *Take heed that ye be not deceived: for many shall come in my name,* saying, I am *Christ*; and the time draweth near: go ye not therefore after them.' (Luke 21:8 KJV, emphasis added)

[4] 'And Jesus answered and said unto them, Take heed that no man deceive you. [5]For many shall come in my name, saying, *'I am Christ;'* and shall deceive many.' (Matt. 24:4-5 KJV, emphasis added)

Now, think about it. Jesus uses the word *you* at least eight times. Yes, the disciples being addressed were Jews (Peter, James, John, and Andrew); however, they would soon be the apostles and fathers of the early church. Remember that the church was initially 100% Jewish. Jesus is warning them not to be deceived. Israel as a nation has not received Jesus as Messiah and will still be deceived at the beginning of the 70th week of Daniel. They will enter into a covenant with the antichrist during that time.

Ponder this. Only followers of Christ are looking for His return. If you are a follower of Christ, you are a member of the body of Christ – the church (whether Jew or Gentile). Followers of

Christ include Messianic Jews (Jews who have accepted Jesus as Messiah) and Gentile believers. If the rapture occurs before events described in the Olivet Discourse, whom could Jesus be addressing? The only people left on earth would be the unbelieving nation of Israel and the unbelieving world. The Messianic Jews would be already gone. This means that there would be no followers of Christ left on earth. The nation of Israel is not looking for the return of Christ. Besides, Israel, as a nation, will not be saved until the end of the 70th week of Daniel. So, how could the Olivet Discourse be addressed to only the nation of Israel? It does not make sense.

Let us look at this in another way. The Olivet Discourse is addressed to those who represent Christ on earth. Matthew 24:9 says, 'Then shall they deliver you up to be afflicted, and shall kill you: and ye shall be hated of all nations for *my name's sake.*' Ponder this question: what prophecy says that Israel, as a nation will be hated for Jesus' name's sake? None. However, the church is and will be hated for Jesus' name's sake.

'Elect' or 'elect's' is mentioned in Matthew 24 (verses 22, 24, and 31) three times. It is also mentioned in Mark 13 (verses 20, 22, and 27) three times. Who are the elect in these verses? Some hold that the elect mentioned in these verses are the believing Jews and Gentiles. I would agree. However, some hold that the elect mentioned here is the nation of Israel. Many pre-tribulaitonist believe this. As a former pre-tribulationist, I was taught the very same thing.

You see, Israel, as a nation, would not be representatives of Christ on earth, nor would they suffer for Christ. Besides, Revelation 12:6 says that the woman (Israel) will flee to a place in the wilderness prepared by God for 3 ½ years ('1260 days'). Revelation 12:13-17 literally says that at the beginning of the great tribulation, the dragon (Satan) will try to persecute the woman (Israel), but will not be able to. Israel will be protected for 3 ½ years. Satan will then make war against the rest of her offspring (the church) who keep the commandment of God and have the testimony of Jesus Christ. Only the church has the testimony of Jesus Christ and will be representatives of Christ on earth. Who is left for Satan to persecute on earth then? Not the unbelieving world, they are already worshipping Satan. Simple reasoning should only lead us to one reasonable answer. It is this elect group mentioned in Matthew 24 which could only be the church (both Messianic Jews and Gentile believers). So, Matthew 24 applies to both the church and Israel.

I know, some of you might say, 'What about the great revival as a result of the preaching of the 144,000 Jewish witnesses?' I was taught this very thing. However, the 144,000 are never called witnesses and Scripture does not paint a picture of a worldwide revival. There will be many great signs and lying wonders, but only the non-elect will be deceived. Even the elect would be deceived if it were possible (Matt. 24:24). Remember, these elect already believe in Christ. Satan will deceive many and God Himself will send some type of strong delusion for many to believe the lie that they might be condemned (2 Thess. 2:9-12). Besides, we find over and over again (in the book of Revelation, during God's wrath) that the unsaved inhabitants of the earth do not repent and that they blaspheme God's name. Let us face it, this *does not* sound like an atmosphere of a great worldwide revival. For more information on this, see chapter 10 (Will There Be a Great Revival after the Rapture?).

What's the Sign of Christ's Coming (*Parousia*)?

The dialog began in the temple area, but the disciples waited until they were alone with Jesus before they privately asked Jesus about the sign of His coming and the end of the age. Jesus' answer to their questions makes up the Olivet Discourse. The questions are found in verse 3 of Matthew 24.

> [3] 'And as he sat upon the mount of Olives, the disciples came unto him privately, saying, Tell us, when shall these things be? and *what shall be the sign of thy coming*, and of *the end of the world (age)*?' (Matt. 24:3 KJV, emphasis added)

The disciples (specifically Peter, James, John, and Andrew) wanted to know the sign of Jesus' coming. The real meaning for 'coming' used here is lost in the English translation. As we saw in chapter 5, the Greek word for *coming* is *parousia* (Strong's #3952), which means *a presence or presence with* (literally *being with*). The word is used as a noun, not a verb. It is an event, which may have other activities within or surrounding it. This does not mean to go or come back and forth. The Greek word for that would be *erchomai* (Strong's #2064), which means *to go or come*. The word *parousia* is used by Paul in the rapture passage (1 Thess. 4:13-17) in verse 15 KJV it says, 'For this we say unto you by the word of the Lord, that we which are alive and remain unto the *coming* of the Lord shall not prevent them which are asleep.' This is referring to the very same event that the disciples asked about here in the Olivet Discourse. The word *parousia* is also used by Paul in 2 Thessalonians 2:1, 'Now we beseech you, brethren, by the *coming* of our Lord Jesus Christ, and *by* our *gathering together* unto him,' and again ties the rapture ('our gathering together') with the *parousia*. So, you would expect the rapture and Christ's *parousia* to be closely tied together. Therefore, a sign should be associated with it. For more detail on the word *parousia* and its biblical uses, review chapter 5.

The Sign of the End of the Age

'And what *shall be* the sign of thy coming, and of *the end of the world (age)?*' (Matt. 24:3b). If you are using a King James Version Bible, it will read 'the end of the world' instead of 'the end of the age.' The word *world* is not a good translation for this particular Greek word. A better translation is *age*. The Greek word is *aion* (Strong's #165) meaning *an age or era.* In Jesus' parable of the wheat and the tares, it says, 'The harvest is the end of the age (Matt. 13:39),' so, Jesus had previously talked about the same event that the disciples asked Him about in the Olivet Discourse. We will find in our text that at the end of the age, there will be a harvest (a gathering together of the wheat [sons of the kingdom] and tares [sons of the wicked one). One might say, 'Wait a minute, I know that parable and it says that the angels gather out the wicked ones. It appears that the righteous are left, but at the rapture the righteous are gathered and the wicked are left.' That is a good point, so let us look at the parable of the dragnet. It is found in Matthew 13:47-50 and it also speaks of the end of the age. It compares the end of the age with a net being thrown into the sea, which gathered every kind (good and bad, without discrimination) into the net; however, the good will be gathered into vessels and the bad will be cast away. Verses 49 and 50 of Matthew 13 KJV say, 'So shall it be *at the end of the world (age): the angels shall come forth, and sever (separate) the wicked from among the just,* and shall cast them (the wicked) into the furnace of fire: there shall be wailing and gnashing of teeth.' Now, we all know that there are no contradictions in Scripture, but there *appears* to be one here. Remember that parables teach spiritual truths. The point is that there will be a separation of the righteous and the wicked at the end of the age. The rapture occurs at the end of the age, and at the rapture, there will be a separation. The righteous will be rescued and the wicked will be judged.

In Matthew 3:7-12, John the Baptist spoke of this future time of the wrath to come. In verse 12 NKJV it says, 'His winnowing fan *is* in His hand, and He will thoroughly clean out His threshing floor, and *gather His wheat into the barn*; but *He will burn up the chaff with unquenchable fire'* (emphasis added). We also find a picture of a harvest here. The wheat (the righteous) will be gathered into the barn and the chaff (the wicked) will be burned. The end of the age is also a time for Christ's coming and the day of the Lord. There are signs associated with the coming of Christ and the end of the age. The sign for the end of the age is the same as the sign associated with the day of the Lord. That occurs *before* the day of the Lord (God's wrath) begins (Joel 2:31; Matt. 24:29). The sign is the divine darkening of the sun, moon, and stars. Simply put, the day of the Lord and the end of the age are one in the same. At the end of the age, the Lord will judge the wicked world.

We saw earlier that the Great Commission (Matt. 28:18-20) is directed to the church. Now, Jesus says something interesting at the end of verse 20 NKJV. He says, 'And lo, I am with you always, *even to the end of the age*' (emphasis added). If Jesus will be with the church up to the end of the age and the rapture occurs at the end of the age (Christ's coming), it could only mean that the church is here on earth until that time (until Christ's coming and the rapture, 1 Thess. 4:15-17). Now, we just saw that God's wrath begins at the end of the age. So, it must be understood that the church will be on earth through most of the events described in the Olivet Discourse (up until Christ's coming). The words *the end* are used in Matthew 24 verses 6, 13, and 14. The words *the end*, in context refer to the end of the age. Notice what is said about the end of the age. Also, notice that the end of the age *does not* occur before the events described in the Olivet Discourse begin.

Matthew 24 – The end

- Verse 6 – 'And ye shall hear of wars and rumours of wars: see that ye be not troubled: for all these things must come to pass, but *the end (the end of the age)* is not yet.' (KJV emphasis added)
- Verse 13 – 'But he that shall endure unto *the end (the end of the age)*, the same shall be saved (physically rescued).' (KJV emphasis added)
- Verse 14 – 'And this gospel of the kingdom shall be preached in all the world for a witness unto all nations; and then shall *the end (the end of the age)* come.' (KJV emphasis added)

In the Jewish mind, there were two ages. The first is *this present age* (which is wicked) and the other is *the age to come* (described in Isaiah 65:17-25 and other places in Scripture) when the Messiah will rule on the earth. In Jesus' day, the Jewish people were looking for the Messiah to rescue them from the Roman rule and set up His kingdom on earth. There did not realize that this age would come later (at Jesus' second coming). At Jesus' first coming, He had to provide a way to rescue us from sin by paying for our sin debt on the cross. At His second coming (*parousia*), those who are alive and trust in Christ will be physically rescued (by way of rapture). Afterwards, God's wrath is poured out on the ungodly, during the day of the Lord, and later the Messianic Kingdom will be set up on earth. The church age separates Jesus' first and second coming. We are in the church age at this time. God is using the church to spread His word. It is a time of God's grace.

The Overview (Up to the End of the Age)

⁴ 'And Jesus answered and said unto them, Take heed that no man deceive you. ⁵For many shall come in my name, saying, I am Christ; and shall deceive many. ⁶And ye shall hear of wars and rumours of wars: see that ye be not troubled: for all *these things* must come to pass, but the end is not yet. ⁷For nation shall rise against nation, and kingdom against kingdom: and there shall be famines, and pestilences, and earthquakes, in divers places. ⁸All these *are* the beginning of sorrows. ⁹Then shall they deliver you up to be afflicted, and shall kill you: and ye shall be hated of all nations for my name's sake. ¹⁰And then shall many be offended, and shall betray one another, and shall hate one another. ¹¹And many false prophets shall rise, and shall deceive many. ¹²And because iniquity shall abound, the love of many shall wax cold. ¹³But he that shall endure unto the end, the same shall be saved. ¹⁴And this gospel of the kingdom shall be preached in all the world for a witness unto all nations; and then shall the end come.' (Matt. 24:4-14 KJV)

Verses 4 through 14 make up an overview of the events that carry us up to the end of the age. This overview covers from the beginning of the 70th week of Daniel to the end of the age. However, the end of the age is not at the end of the 70th week of Daniel. Then, in verse 15, Jesus will refer to events described within this overview. He will refer to the middle of the 70th week of Daniel (when the abomination of desolation [Dan. 9:27] and the great tribulation begins) and will carry us up to the gathering together (the rapture) of the elect at the end of the age. We find this in verses 15 through 31. We already saw that the harvest is at the end of the age and the church will be here until the end of the age. So, we can obviously expect to rapture to take place at the end of the age.

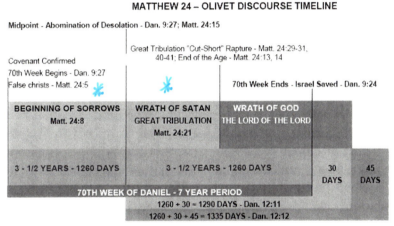

The 24th chapter of Matthew first gives an overview and then gives details of the events. We find the same thing in Genesis 1 and 2. Chapter one is an overview of creation, but the second chapter focuses on the creation of man, giving more detail of what happened during that time.

Jesus starts out with a warning to the disciples not to be deceived in verse 4 and warning them again in verses 24 and 25 of Matthew 24. Concerning the same events surrounding the coming (*parousia*) of Christ, Paul tells the Thessalonians not to be deceived (2 Thess. 2:3). There will obviously be much deception in the last days (verses 11, 23, 24, and 26 of Matthew 24). Next, Jesus mentions false christs that *will* deceive many people (v 5). Then, He mentions that people will 'hear of wars and rumors of wars' (v 6). Even at that, Jesus says, '*See that ye be not troubled*: *for all these things must come to pass, but the end is not yet.* For nation shall rise against nation, and kingdom against kingdom: and there shall be famines, and pestilences, and earthquakes, in divers places. *All these are the beginning of sorrows'* (verses 6-8 KJV emphasis added). Although there will be false christs, wars and rumors of wars, even famine and pestilences, and earthquakes, Jesus says not to be troubled, 'the end,' meaning 'the end of the age' is not yet; it is just the beginning of sorrows. The Greek word used here for *sorrows* is *odin* (Strong's #5604), which means *a pang* or *throe,* literally *childbirth pain.* So, comparing these events to the birth of a child, they are only the beginning – not even hard labor yet. Clearly, Jesus does not even call these events tribulation; they are merely called the beginning of birth pains. At this point, the world is *not* falling apart at the seams. More specifically the events associated with the beginning of birth pains appear to be everyday events. Yes, that means that the first 3 ½ years are somewhat normal in many ways. The sign of the coming (*parousia*) of Christ comes later (verses 29-30). Up to this point, the antichrist has not caused the abomination that causes desolation yet (which begins his persecution of the elect [the great tribulation]), which he does at the 3 ½-year point (Dan. 9:27).

You will find that if you compare the events from the Olivet Discourse with the events in the 6th chapter of Revelation, they fit almost perfectly and fall in the very same order. Just in case you are unfamiliar with the 6th chapter of the book of Revelation, I will give you a brief outline. In the 5th chapter of the book of Revelation, we find a scroll written on the inside and outside and sealed with seven seals on it (Rev. 5:1). Only the Lamb (Jesus Christ) was worthy to break the seals on the scroll to look at it. In the 6th chapter of Revelation, six of the seven seals are broken. As each seal is broken, something happens on the earth. The events that occur, as each seal is broken can be compared with the different events described in the Olivet Discourse (Matthew 24). For your convenience, I have proved a chart in this chapter making that comparison.

Before we get to this chart, there is something that I must discuss. As a former pre-tribulationist, I was taught that since the seals were being opened by the Lamb of God (Jesus Christ) in the

6th chapter of Revelation, the events that followed as each seal was broken was the wrath of God. However, I have since learned that this cannot be the case. God's wrath does not begin until after the 6th seal is broken. I will explain.

One very important reason is that Scripture clearly says that the day of the Lord does not begin until after a divine darkening of the sun, moon, and stars (Joel 2:31; Acts 2:19-20). These sign does not occur until after the 6th seal is broken. So, any events before these sign cannot be God's wrath. After all, there are no contradictions in Scripture.

Contrary to what one might believe, the seals were on the outside of the scroll. I was initially taught that one seal was on the outside and when it was broken, the scroll would be opened a little ways until the next seal was reached. It sounded somewhat strange when I first heard it, but I did not really question it. A scroll with seven seals was actually found, but the seals were all on the outside of the scroll. In 1962, one was discovered in a cave north of Jericho. The American School of Oriental Research purchased it. The seals were cut. It contained twelve lines of Aramaic script. The scroll was a legal document recording the sale of a slave named Yehohanan. It was dated March 18, 335 BC. A seven-sealed scroll would be an important legal document. John having seen a seven sealed scroll would immediately know this.

Before a seal could be broken on a scroll, a condition must be met. Not just anyone could break open the seals on a scroll. Just as there are conditions that must be met to break the seals on a scroll, conditions must be met on earth before the return of Christ. At the 5th seal, when the martyred souls under the altar ask God when will His wrath be poured out on the ungodly (on earth) to avenge their blood, God tells them, not until a certain number of their brethren are martyred (Rev. 6:9-11). The martyrs that cry out for God to avenge their blood realize that God's wrath has not begun yet.

There is also the argument that this is not a request for church-age saints, because it was not the request of Stephen a martyr of the early church (Acts 8:54-60). As Stephen was being stoned, he asked the Lord not to charge those who were stoning him with that sin (Acts 8:60). However, we must remember that God has already said that there would be a time when He will pour out His wrath on earth. This is clear throughout Scripture. See chapter 7 in this book on Thessalonians (read the section on 2 Thessalonians 1).

Angels are the instruments used during the day of the Lord to pour out God's wrath upon the wicked who dwell on earth (during the trumpet and bowl judgments). However, the angels are not directly involved as Christ breaks the seals. As we said earlier, at the breaking of the 6th seal, the sign associated with the day of the Lord occurs (i.e. divine darkening of the sun, moon, and stars). The openings of the seals parallel the events described in Matthew 24. The following chart will make these comparisons. In Matthew, concerning the events preceding the coming of Christ, Jesus said, 'All these things must come to pass.' In so many words this means that certain conditions must be met before the return of Christ. This is precisely what we find as each seal is opened in the 6th chapter of Revelation.

COMPARING SCRIPTURE WITH SCRIPTURE

The Olivet Discourse in Matthew 24, Mark 13, and The 7 Seals in Revelation 6, 7, & 8

Matt. 24	Mark 13	The Olivet Discourse	Revelation		
V 5	V 8	FALSE CHRISTS	ANTICHRIST (White Horse)	1st Seal	6:1-2
VV 6-7a	V 7	WARS/RUMORS	CONFLICTS/WARS (Red Horse)	2nd Seal	6:3-4
V 7	V 8	FAMINE	FAMINE (Black Horse)	3rd Seal	6:5-6
V 9, 21	V 19	"THE GREAT TRIBULATION BEGINS-Persecution of the elect"			
V 9	V 12	DEATH	DEATH/HADES (Pale Horse)	4th Seal	6:7-8
V 9-10		MARTYRDOM	MARTYRED SOULS	5th Seal	6:9-11
V 29	VV 24-26	COSMIC DISTURBANCES (Sun, Moon, and Stars)	COSMIC DISTURBANCES (Sun, Moon, and Stars)	6th Seal	6:12-17
V 30		"THE "SIGN" OF CHRIST'S COMING SEEN IN HEAVEN"			
V 30		"THE COMING (*Parousia*) OF CHRIST"			
VV 29-31	VV 24-27	THE GATHERING OF THE ELECT (The Rapture)	GREAT MULTITUDE IN HEAVEN (Out of the Great Tribulation, before God's wrath begins)		7:9-14
VV 14, 37-39		THE WRATH OF GOD BEGINS (The End of the Age)	THE WRATH OF GOD BEGINS	7th Seal	8:1-7

Matthew 24, verse 9 mentions *tribulation* and verse 21 mentions *great tribulation*. Because of this, many break the 70th week of Daniel into two parts, the first 3 ½ years are usually called the tribulation period and the last 3 ½ years are usually called the great tribulation period. However, when one compares the Olivet Discourse with the 6th chapter of Revelation, you will find that the first three seals should actually be called the beginning of birth pains, which takes us up to the 3 ½-year point. Again, according to Jesus, the first 3 ½ years appear to be somewhat normal. However, the persecution usually associated with the great tribulation does not occur until the 4th seal (Rev. 6:7-8), which should be compared with verse 9 of Matthew 24.

Verse 9 KJV says, 'Then *shall they deliver you up to be afflicted, and shall kill you: and ye shall be hated of all nations for my name's sake.*' The NKJV says, 'Then *they will deliver you up to tribulation* and *kill you,* and *you will be hated by all nations for My name's sake.*' The word *tribulation* mentioned here in verse 9 is describing the same events as 'the great tribulation' mentioned in verse 21. Verses 9 through 12 describe what happens during this time of great tribulation; while verses 15 through 21 give a warning and instructions for those who live in Judea to flee when they see the abomination of desolation, a sign that the great tribulation is about to begin. Judea is Jerusalem and the territory immediately surrounding it. Although the great tribulation begins in Jerusalem, against the nation of Israel (verses 15-16), we find followers of Christ (Christians) undergoing great pressure, being killed and hated because of their identification with Christ (v 9). This tribulation or great tribulation comes *from* the antichrist (Rev. 12:17; 13:7), not from God.

The Greek word for *tribulation* is *thlipsis* (Strong's #2347), which means *pressure, affliction, persecution, or trouble.* Picture a huge stone or great weight on someone that slowly squeezes the life out of him or her. That is *thlipsis.* The tribulation will be *cut short* and will not go to the end of the 70th week of Daniel. This is a very important fact to keep in mind. God will rescue His own before His wrath begins, which is reserved for the wicked (1 Thess. 1:10; *2 Peter 2:9). We (the saints) are not appointed to

Gods wrath

God's wrath (Rom. 5:9; 1 Thess. 5:9). God's wrath will be poured out during the day of the Lord.

Verse 10 of Matthew 24 NKJV says, 'And then shall many be *offended,* and shall betray one another, and shall hate one another.' The Greek word for *offended* is *skandalizo* (Strong's #4624), which means to *entice to sin or to make to offend.* According to Paul (in 2 Thessalonians 2:1-3), the coming of Christ, the rapture and day of the Lord will not come unless '*the falling away comes first,* and the *man of sin is revealed.*' The Greek word for *falling away* is *apostasia* (Strong's #646); it means a *defection or revolt,* a literal *defection from the truth, apostasy.* The timing on these two Scriptures parallels each other. We can see that the antichrist will be revealed and the apostasy occurs *before* the rapture.

False prophets will deceive many (Matt. 24:11; Rev. 13:11-17). Lawlessness will abound and the love of many will grow cold (Matt. 24:12). The lack of love leads to lawlessness. The apostle John addresses love in 1 John 2:3-6, 9-11; 3:14-15, and verse 23. John makes it clear that he who loves his brother abides in the light, and he who hates, walks in darkness.

He Who Endures to the End of the Age Will Be Delivered

Matthew 24, verses 13 and 14 are difficult for many people to understand. Verse 13 KJV says, 'But he that shall endure *unto the end,* the same shall be s*aved.*' Now, those who have any type of understanding of the doctrine of salvation might say in reference to verse 13, 'Aren't we saved by grace through faith apart from works (Gal. 2:16; Eph. 2:8)?' The answer is, 'Yes, you are right.' One might then say, 'What is this business about enduring to the end to be saved?' The meaning of these verses is found in the context of the persecution of those who are identified with Christ. Keep in mind that there is great persecution going on at this time. This persecution is against the elect (those who name the name of Christ). They are enduring great pressure (being killed, imprisoned, and hated by all for the sake of Christ). The Greek word for *endure* is *hupomeno* (Strong's #5278), which means to *stay or remain under, to bear trials or have fortitude, persevere.* 'The end' in context is the end of the age. So, those who remain under pressure until the end of the age will be delivered.

The Greek word for *saved* is *sozo*. When used as a noun, it is *soteria* (Strong's #4982) meaning *save or deliver*. In context, the word *saved* means *delivered*. Being saved can either be referring to spiritual salvation, which occurs the moment that you believe (Eph. 1:13, 14) or physical deliverance, as in being rescued (1 Thess. 4:15-17; 2 Thess. 1:6-8). The same Greek word, *sozo*, is used for physical deliverance in Matt. 8:25; Mark 13:20; Luke 23:35; and John 12:27. Since those mentioned in the Olivet Discourse being persecuted are genuine Christians, they already have a spiritual salvation. However, they are looking for a *physical deliverance* that will come at the end of the age, at the harvest (Matt. 13:39). This is when God will rescue (rapture) the righteous from persecution *before* His wrath begins. Regarding the rapture, 1 Thessalonians 4:17 KJV says, 'Then we which are *alive* and *remain* shall be caught up together with them in the clouds, to meet the Lord in the air: and so shall we ever be with the Lord' (emphasis added). The Greek word for *remain*, literally means, *survive*. So, it could be read, 'Then we which are *alive* and *survive* shall be caught up...' So, he who is 'alive and *survives*' until Christ's coming (at the end of the age) will be *physically delivered* (*raptured*). Jesus said, 'Blessed *are* they which are persecuted for righteousness' sake: for theirs is the kingdom of heaven' (Matt. 5:10). Christ will return during a great persecution on earth, and those who survive until His coming will be rescued at His coming.

Matthew 24, verse 14 KJV says, '*And this gospel of the kingdom shall be preached in all the world for a witness unto all nations; and then shall the end come*' (emphasis added). Many think that Christ will not or cannot return until the gospel is preached throughout the world through Christian evangelism. Now, the gospel *should* be preached throughout the world, but verse 14 is *not* saying that unless we do it, Christ will not come. The gospel spoken of in this verse is the gospel of the kingdom, not the gospel of Christ. That is not a play on words. The two are *not* the same. I will give a brief explanation.

The word *gospel*, comes from the Greek word *euaggelion* (Strong's # 2098), meaning *a good message*. During the time that Jesus spoke these words, any good news was considered the gospel. Today, when we hear the word *gospel*, we normally think of the message of the death, burial, and resurrection of Christ. This message is called the gospel of Christ. However, this was not the case in Jesus' day. It was some 30 years after the death, burial, and resurrection of Christ (during the Apostle Paul's ministry) that the word *gospel* (*euaggelion*) began to take on the meaning that we use today. Paul wrote in 1 Corinthians 15:1-4, 'Moreover, brethren, I declare unto you the *gospel which I preached unto you*, which also ye have received, and wherein ye stand; *By which also ye are saved*, if ye keep in memory what I preached unto you, unless ye have believed in vain. For I delivered unto you first of all that which I also received, how that *Christ died for our sins according to the scriptures; And that he was buried, and that he rose again the third day according to the scriptures...*' (emphasis added) The gospel of the kingdom is not the same message as the gospel of Christ. The word *kingdom* comes from the Greek word *basiliea* (Strong's #932), meaning *rule* or *realm*. In context, it means the rule or reign of God. So, the gospel of the kingdom is a literal message of the reign of God. It also contains a warning of the judgment of God upon the ungodly, as John the Baptist preached (Matt. 3:1-12; Luke 3:7-17). In Matthew, we read of Jesus preaching the gospel of the kingdom (Matt. 4:23; 9:35).

The kingdom of God is the kingdom of light. There is no darkness at all in the kingdom of God. Satan's kingdom is the kingdom of darkness. Like it or not, each human being is in one kingdom or the other. There is obviously much darkness in this world today, just like there was in Jesus' day. The world is blind to the future judgment to come, just as it is blind to the saving grace found in Jesus Christ, paid for by His death, burial, and resurrection. As just mentioned, this saving grace is presented in the gospel of Christ. Before we can understand what it is to be saved, we need to understand what we are being saved from. The gospel of the kingdom sheds light on this. It warns us that God's judgment is coming. With this news, we must make a decision.

Turn to Christ and be saved or face the wrath of God.

An interesting phrase is found twice in the book of Matthew (Matt. 4:17; 16:21), the phrase is *'from that time Jesus began.'* This is a technical phrase, which means that Jesus had not done it before that moment. Matthew 4:17 KJV says, *'From that time Jesus began* to preach, and to say, 'Repent, for the kingdom of heaven is at hand.'' This was when Jesus began his earthly ministry. He began to preach the gospel of the kingdom. Jesus did not mention the gospel of Christ (His death, burial, and resurrection) until after Peter's confession at Caesarea Philippi. Peter said he believed that Jesus was the Son of the Living God. We find all of this in Matthew 16:13-23. After Peter's confession, we find the second time that the phrase was used (Matt. 16:21). Matthew 16:21 KJV says, *'From that time forth began* Jesus to show unto his disciples, how that he must go unto Jerusalem, and suffer many things of the elders and chief priests and scribes, and be killed, and be raised again the third day.' Jesus had not disclosed this to the disciples previously. This was a new message from Jesus. We know this was a new message because of Peter's reaction to what Jesus had just said. Peter was shocked. Had this been the gospel of the kingdom, Peter would not have reacted as he did.

In the context of the gospel being preached in the entire world before Jesus returns (Matt. 24:14), we can find who is preaching it in the book of Revelation.

> [6] 'And I saw another *angel fly in the midst of heaven, having the everlasting gospel to preach unto them that dwell on the earth, and to every nation, and kindred, and tongue, and people,* [7]Saying with a loud voice, *Fear God, and give glory to him; for the hour of his judgment is come: and worship him that made heaven, and earth, and the sea, and the fountains of waters.'* (Rev. 14:6-7 KJV, emphasis added)

> [9] 'And the third angel followed them, saying with a loud voice, If any man worship the beast and his image, and

receive his mark in his forehead, or in his hand, [10]The same shall drink of the wine of the wrath of God, which is poured out without mixture into the cup of his indignation; and he shall be tormented with fire and brimstone in the presence of the holy angels, and in the presence of the Lamb: [11]And the smoke of their torment ascendeth up for ever and ever: and they have no rest day nor night, who worship the beast and his image, and whosoever receiveth the mark of his name.' (Rev. 14: 9-11 KJV)

It is easy to see that the gospel of the kingdom that Jesus is speaking of comes from an angel. The final worldwide gospel message preached by the angel is simple and to the point. 'Fear God and give Him glory.' A third angel warns the world about the consequences of worshipping the beast (antichrist) and receiving his mark. Eternal condemnation is the consequences. The end, i.e. 'the end of the age,' will come sometime after this final gospel of the kingdom is preached. As stated throughout this book, the rapture and the second coming of Christ occur simultaneously at the end of the age.

Verse 14 completes the overview of the end of the age. Next, Jesus will refer to a specific event spoken of by Daniel that will occur before the end of the age. He will go back to what will happen at the middle of the 70th week of Daniel (3 ½-year point) and give a warning concerning this time.

The Great Tribulation

[15] 'When ye therefore shall see the abomination of desolation, spoken of by Daniel the prophet, stand in the holy place, (whoso readeth, let him understand:) [16]Then let them which be in Judaea flee into the mountains: [17]Let him which is on the housetop not come down to take any thing out of his house: [18]Neither let him which is in the field return back to take his clothes. [19]And woe unto them that are with child, and to them that give suck in those days!

[20]But pray ye that your flight be not in the winter, neither on the sabbath day: [21]For then shall be great tribulation, such as was not since the beginning of the world to this time, no, nor ever shall be. [22]And except those days should be shortened, there should no flesh be saved: but for the elect's sake those days shall be shortened.' (Matt. 24:15-22 KJV)

In light of the overview in verses 4 through 14, beginning at verse 15, Jesus gives a warning about an event that will trigger the great tribulation. This event (the great tribulation) is described as tribulation in verse 9 and great tribulation in verse 21. The great tribulation time period is limited to the midpoint of the 70th week of Daniel until the second coming of Christ. The midpoint of the 70th week of Daniel is when the antichrist, who is empowered by Satan, begins his persecution of the saints, which begins the wrath of Satan (Dan. 9:27; Rev. 12:12, 17; 13:5-8). Remember that up through verse 8 of Matthew 24, He is describing only the beginning of birth pains, which Jesus says not to be troubled about, because they must come to pass (v 6) before the end of the age. The warning and instructions in verses 15 through 22 literally belong between verses 8 and 9 if you want to read these events chronologically. This is not necessarily uncommon. For instance, the book of Daniel is not written in chronological order. The major sections of the book of Revelation are in chronological order. By this, I mean the breaking of the seals, which are followed by the trumpet and then bowl judgments. However, there are sections of that which do not fall into chronological order. For instance, after God's wrath begins at the first trumpet judgment (Rev. 8:7), we read of Satan being thrown from heaven and the persecution of believers in Revelation 12:7 through chapter 13:8. These events clearly occurred before the wrath of God began. They describe events that occurred between the 4th and 6th seals from chapter 6 of Revelation. Now, I do not mean that we should just read prophetic books (or any Scripture for that matter) and then cut and paste different sections as we please to fit whatever view we hold. Our goal should always be is to uncover the truth.

The abomination of desolation spoken of by Daniel (v 15) can be found recorded in Daniel 9:27. It speaks of when the antichrist will desecrate the temple by committing an abominable sin against God that causes the temple to be desolate in the middle of the 70th week of Daniel. Now, at the time of this writing (the writing of this book, that is), Jerusalem does not have a temple. So, obviously there has to be a temple built in Jerusalem before there can be one there to be defiled by the antichrist. This temple could possibly be something as simple as a tabernacle (tent) like the one at the time of Moses through King David.

At the sight of the abomination, Jesus warns those in Jerusalem to flee into the mountains. (Most believe that they will flee to Petra, an area southeast of Jerusalem and approximately 60 miles north of the Gulf of Aquabah-near the Red Sea). However, Revelation 12:13-17 says they (the woman, meaning Israel or a remnant of Israel) will be protected for 3 ½ years. It appears that they will receive some type of supernatural protection from God. Verse 17 NKJV of Revelation 12 says, 'And the dragon (Satan) was enraged with the woman (Israel), and he went to make war with the rest of her offspring, who keep the commandments of God and have the testimony of Jesus Christ (the 'true' church).' The 'true' church is the only body of people who have the testimony of Jesus Christ. At that time, the church will then experience the wrath of Satan during the great tribulation. The reason that they are described as the 'true church' is to separate them from those who merely claim to be a part of the church. All who claim to be part of the church or body of Christ are not. Only the 'true church' will not deny Christ.

Verses 17 and 18 speak of the urgency, for those who love the living God, to leave Jerusalem and the surrounding area. Jesus told them not to even go back to get a coat if they are not at home. Children will slow the women down and both the mother and child's life will be in danger (v 19). Just as the witness to Jesus Christ spread from Jerusalem, to all of Judea and Samaria, and to the end of the earth (Acts 1:8b), so will the persecution that begins in Jerusalem, spread throughout the world.

Verse 20 NKJV says, 'And pray that your flight may not be in winter or on the Sabbath.' Why not in the winter or on the Sabbath? Well, if you have no coat, you will simply freeze during the winter nights in the desert. In the desert, even if it is warm during the day, it will be cold at night. Now, this mention of the Sabbath is one of the reasons why many say that the church is not here during this time, because the church worships on Sunday, not on Saturday. Yes, it is true that under the Jewish law, one was only allowed to travel a Sabbath's day journey (approximately 1000 yards), which is between a half and three quarters of a mile. Of course, the church is not under the law, but under grace. However, Israel's airline, El Al, which flies out of Tel Aviv has *no* flights that leave Tel Aviv on a Saturday (Sabbath) even to this day. No Jewish buses run on the Sabbath. As the Orthodox or Ultra Orthodox Jews gain power, it is very possible that no vehicles will be allowed to travel in or out of Jerusalem, whether public or private transportation. If that is the case, and if they try to leave Israel in haste on a Sabbath during this future time, it will have to be by foot. This of course would be a hindrance for those who are trying to escape the great tribulation.

Jesus said that these days of great tribulation (Satan's wrath) would be shortened (cut-short). The great tribulation begins after the 3 ½-year point of the 70th week of Daniel. That means that some time between the 3 ½-year point and the end of the 70th week of Daniel, the great tribulation ends. 'And except those *days should be shortened*, there should no flesh be saved: but for the elect's sake those days shall be shortened' (verse 22 KJV, emphasis added). The Greek word for *shortened* is, *koloboo*, (Strong's #2856), which means to *amputate or shorten.* In the Greek here, the action happens to the subject. What is the subject? It is the 'great tribulation.' Jesus says that this period (the great tribulation, not the 70th week of Daniel) will be cut-short for the elect's sake (Matt. 24:22; Mark 13:20), more than likely because the persecution against the elect will be so great. So *being that the tribulation period is cut-short and does not go to the end of the 70th week of Daniel*, it is not unreasonable to see Matthew 24:29-31 as a picture of the rapture. The rapture is what cuts short the great tribulation. The nation of Israel or much of the nation of Israel is protected in the wilderness and the church is now removed from earth by the rapture. With no one to persecute, the tribulation is cut short. In so many words, this means that the rapture will occur some time after the 3 ½-year point. Immediately after the rapture comes God's wrath. So we have the great tribulation (Satan's wrath), then the rapture (gathering together) and afterwards God's wrath.

History Will Repeat Itself (Maccebees)

We all know that there is much to learn from history. Many times it repeats itself. I believe that there is much to learn from an event that took place some 160 or so years before the birth of Christ (168 to 165B.C.). During this time, thousands from Israel died under the abominable rule of Antiochus Epiphanes. He was a Syrian king who desecrated the temple in Jerusalem, caused Israel to be desolate, and with threat of death, made many in Israel forsake God and His Laws. The rule of the antichrist to come will resemble the rule of Antiochus Epiphanes' from the past. Note that one family made a stand against him. This was the family of Mattathias (a priest) and his sons. The account is recorded in the books of 1 & 2 Maccabees of the Apocrypha. 1st & 2nd Maccabees make up the most important and possibly the most reliable historical writing in the Apocrypha. They are the primary source of history from 180 to 134B.C. It talks about the work that God did through Mattathias and his sons in order to bring deliverance to Israel from Antiochus Epiphanes.

The Apocrypha contains recorded historical accounts from the inter-testament period between Malachi (the last Old Testament book) and Matthew (the first New Testament book). Although the apocryphal books did not attain canonical status (because they did not meet the rule of acceptable status to be considered as Scripture), they are considered historically accurate and can be found in a Roman Catholic Bible. Apocrypha means *to hide from or keep secret.* When Jesus warned the disciples of the abomination of desolation, their minds probably wondered back to this horrible time in Israel's history (when Antiochus Epiphanes ruled) and they probably gasped when Jesus said these words about this as yet future time of tribulation, 'For then shall be great tribulation, such as was not since the beginning of the world to this time, no, nor ever shall be' (Matt. 24:21 KJV).

For your convenience, I have included some of the accounts from 1 Maccabees. Hopefully, it will give you a feel for a small part of what went on during that time. The two sections are entitled 'Installation of Gentile Cults' and 'Pagan Worship Refused.' These verses are from The New Revised Standard Version of the Bible with Apocrypha. I have also included a chart that I made which compares some of the accounts mentioned by Jesus in the Olivet Discourse with the historical accounts recorded in this book from 1st Maccabees.

Installation of Gentile Cults

[41] 'Then the king wrote to his whole kingdom that all should be one people, [42]and that all should give up their particular customs. [43]All the Gentiles accepted the command of the king. Many even from Israel gladly adopted his religion; they sacrificed to idols and profaned the sabbath. [44]And the king sent letters by messengers to Jerusalem and the towns of Judah; he directed them to follow customs strange to the land, [45]to forbid burnt offerings and sacrifices and drink offerings in the sanctuary, to profane sabbaths and festivals, [46]to defile the sanctuary and the priests, [47]to build altars and sacred precincts and shrines for idols, to sacrifice swine and other unclean animals, [48]and to leave their sons uncircumcised. They were to make themselves abominable by everything unclean and profane, [49]so that they would forget the law and change all the ordinances. [50]He added, 'And whoever does not obey the command of the king shall die.'

[51]In such words he wrote to his whole kingdom. He appointed inspectors over all the people and commanded

the towns of Judah to offer sacrifice, town by town. [52]Many of the people, everyone who forsook the law, joined them, and they did evil in the land; [53]they drove Israel into hiding in every place of refuge they had.

[54]Now on the fifteenth day of Chislev, in the one hundred forty-fifth year, they erected a desolating sacrilege on the altar of burnt offering. They also built altars in the surrounding towns of Judah, [55]and offered incense at the doors of the houses and in the streets. [56]The books of the law that they found they tore to pieces and burned with fire. [57]Anyone found possessing the book of the covenant, or anyone who adhered to the law, was condemned to death by decree of the king. [58]They kept using violence against Israel, against those who were found month after month in the towns. [59]On the twenty-fifth day of the month they offered sacrifice on the altar that was on top of the altar of burnt offering. [60]According to the decree, they put to death the women who had their children circumcised, [61]and their families and those who circumcised them; and they hung the infants from their mothers' necks.

[62]But many in Israel stood firm and were resolved in their hearts not to eat unclean food. [63]They chose to die rather than to be defiled by food or to profane the holy covenant; and they did die. [64]Very great wrath came upon Israel.' (1 Maccabees 1:42-64 *The New Revised Standard Version of Bible with Apocrypha*) [1]

Pagan Worship Refused

[15] 'The king's officers who were enforcing the apostasy came to the town of Modein to make them offer sacrifice. [16]Many from Israel came to them; and Mattathias and his sons were assembled. [17]Then the king's officers spoke to Mattathias as follows: 'You are a leader, honored and great in this town, and supported by sons and brothers. [18]Now be the first to come and do what the king commands, as all the

Gentiles and the people of Judah and those that are left in Jerusalem have done. Then you and your sons will be numbered among the Friends of the king, and you and your sons will be honored with silver and gold and many gifts.'

[19]But Mattathias answered and said in a loud voice: 'Even if all the nations that live under the rule of the king obey him, and have chosen to obey his commandments, everyone of them abandoning the religion of their ancestors, [20]I and my sons and my brothers will continue to live by the covenant of our ancestors. [21]Far be it from us to desert the law and the ordinances. [22]We will not obey the king's words by turning aside from our religion to the right hand or to the left.'

[23]When he had finished speaking these words, a Jew came forward in the sight of all to offer sacrifice on the altar in Modein, according to the king's command. [24]When Mattathias saw it, he burned with zeal and his heart was stirred. He gave vent to righteous anger; he ran and killed him on the altar. [25]At the same time he killed the king's officer who was forcing them to sacrifice, and he tore down the altar. [26]Thus he burned with zeal for the law, just as Phinehas did against Zimri son of Salu.

[27]Then Mattathias cried out in the town with a loud voice, saying: 'Let every one who is zealous for the law and supports the covenant come out with me!' [28]Then he and his sons fled to the hills and left all that they had in the town.

[29]At that time many who were seeking righteousness and justice went down to the wilderness to live there, [30]they, their sons, their wives, and their livestock, because troubles pressed heavily upon them. [31]And it was reported to the king's officers, and to the troops in Jerusalem the city of David, that those who had rejected the king's command had gone down to the hiding places in the wilderness. [32]Many pursued them, and overtook them; they encamped opposite them and prepared for battle against them on the sabbath day. [33]They said to them, 'Enough of this! Come

out and do what the king commands, and you will live.'
[34]But they said, 'We will not come out, nor will we do what
the king commands and so profane the sabbath day.' [35]Then
the enemy quickly attacked them. [36]But they did not answer
them or hurl a stone at them or block up their hiding places,
[37]for they said, 'Let us all die in our innocence; heaven and
earth testify for us that you are killing us unjustly.' [38]So
they attacked them on the sabbath, and they died, with their
wives and children and livestock, to the number of a
thousand persons.

[39]When Mattathias and his friends learned of it, they
mourned for them deeply. [40]And all said to their neighbors:
'If we all do as our kindred have done and refuse to fight
with the Gentiles for our lives and for our ordinances, they
will quickly destroy us from the earth.' [41]So they made this
decision that day: 'Let us fight against anyone who comes
to attack us on the sabbath day; let us not all die as our
kindred died in their hiding places.'" (1 Maccabees 2:15-41
*The New Revised Standard Version of Bible with
Apocrypha*)

It is easy the see the similarities of the events described in the
Olivet Discourse and the historial events recorded in the
Maccabees. Hopefully including some of these accounts from the
book of Maccabees was helpful to you.

There was a triumphant ending to the events described in the
Maccabees. Three years to the day of the abomination of the
temple, the Jews were able to re-dedicate their temple on the 25th
of the Jewish month Chislev. This month is equivalent to the
month of December. The temple had to be cleansed and re-
dedicated. Tradition says that at the time of the cleansing of the
temple, only enough olive oil (approved for the temple lampstand)
for one day's use could be found. However, it lasted for eight
whole days. This Dedication Day is now called Hanukkah, which
means *rededication.* It was an eight-day celebration that was
celebrated in Jesus' day (John 10:22) and, still is today.

COMPARING THE OLIVET DISCOURSE WITH 1ˢᵗ MACCABEES

The Olivet Discourse in Matthew 24 and The Inter-Testament History in 1st Maccabees

Matthew 24	Future Abomination in Israel	Historical Abomination in Israel	1 Maccabees
V 15	THE ABOMINATION OF DESOLATION	A DESOLATING SACRILEGE	1:54, 59
V 16	FLEE TO THE MOUNTAINS	ISRAEL INTO HIDING; FLED TO HILLS	1:53; 2:27-29
V 20	PRAY FLIGHT NOT ON THE SABBATH	THEY ATTACKED THEM ON THE SABBATH	2:32-38
V 19	WOE TO THOSE PREGNANT & NURSING IN THOSE DAYS	THEY PUT TO DEATH THE WOMEN THEIR CIRCUMCISED CHILDREN	1:60-61
V 9	THEY WILL KILL YOU	WHOEVER DOES NOT OBEY KING SHALL DIE; MANY DIED RATHER THAN BE DEFILED	1:50, 60-63
V 10	MANY WILL BE OFFENDED (ENTICED TO SIN, APOSTASY)	LETTER FROM KING TO GIVE UP CUSTOMS; MANY ADOPTED KING'S RELIGION & SACRIFICED TO IDOLS	1:41-52
V 9; V21	TRIBULATION; GREAT TRIBULATION	TROUBLE PRESSED HEAVILY UPON THEM; GREAT WRATH	1:64; 2:30

Don't Be Deceived

[23] 'Then if any man shall say unto you, Lo, here *is* Christ, or there; believe *it* not. [24]For there shall arise false Christs, and false prophets, and shall show great signs and wonders; insomuch that, if *it were* possible, they shall deceive the very elect. [25]Behold, I have told you before. [26]Wherefore if they shall say unto you, Behold, he is in the desert; go not forth: behold, *he is* in the secret chambers; believe *it* not. [27]For as the lightning cometh out of the east, and shineth even unto the west; so shall also the coming of the Son of man be. [28]For wheresoever the carcase is, there will the eagles be gathered together.' (Matt. 24:23-28 KJV)

Jesus previously spoke of false christs (v 5) and false prophets (v 11) who will deceive many. He picks this thought up again in verses 23 through 27. The false christs and false prophets will show great signs and wonders, but should not be believed or followed. What is so amazing is that these signs and wonders will be so convincing that they could fool the elect, if it were possible (v 24). Basically, Jesus is telling us beforehand not to believe anyone claiming to have seen Christ. Verse 27 describes what the coming (*parousia*) of the Son of man (Jesus) will be like: 'As lightning comes from the east and flashes to the west.' It is interesting to note that God's glory departed from west to east when leaving the temple (Ezekiel 10-11). The temple was west of the Mount of Olives. The glory of the Lord moved from the temple and departed (east) toward the Mount of Olives (Ezekiel 10:4, 18-19; 11:23). However, at the return of Christ, it appears that Jesus will return from east to west in great glory (verses 27, 30). Verse 28 KJV is somewhat strange. 'For wheresoever the carcase is, there will the eagles be gathered together.' Yes, judgment of the wicked does come with the day of the Lord. The ungodly will receive God's wrath and ultimately be destroyed. Yet, it also refers to a well-known sign to that region. When you see eagles or vultures gathering together, you know there is something dead nearby. No one will have to tell you. Look for and know the sign. Christ's coming (*parousia*) will be sudden and has a specific sign associated with it (Matt. 24:29-30). Look for its sign.

The Coming (*Parousia*) of Christ

[29]'Immediately after the tribulation of those days the sun will be darkened, and the moon will not give its light; the stars will fall from heaven, and the powers of the heavens will be shaken. [30]Then the sign of the Son of Man will appear in heaven, and then all the tribes of the earth will mourn, and they will see the Son of Man coming on the clouds of heaven with power and great glory. [31]And He will send His angels with a great sound of a trumpet, and they will gather together His elect from the four winds, from one end of heaven to the other.' (Matt. 24:29-31 NKJV)

There is a tremendous amount of confusion on this portion of Scripture, especially concerning its timing and the event that it is describing. It occurs immediately after the tribulation. A look at this verse alone would make most say, 'Immediately after the tribulation is the end of the seven-year tribulation period.' However, that would not be accurate. Remember, we saw in verse 22 that the tribulation will be cut short. This means that it will *not* go to the end of the 70th week of Daniel (or the end of the seven-year period to come). The great tribulation begins at the 3 ½-year point of the seven-year period and continues until the coming (*parousia*) of Christ. The great tribulation is when the wrath of Satan is poured out on the nation of Israel (Rev. 12:13-16) and those who have the testimony of Jesus Christ (the church - Rev. 12:17), the saints (Rev. 13:7), or the elect (Matt. 24:22, 31). Those who hold the testimony of Jesus Christ will be delivered (raptured) at the coming of Christ.

Immediately after the tribulation, we find the sun darkened. And since the moon has no light of its own, but only reflects the light from the sun, it will not have light to reflect. Therefore, it will be darkened also. There will be darkness and cosmic disturbances. This is obviously associated with the sign of the day of the Lord. The coming of Christ will follow. These things must occur *before* the day of the Lord can come. 'The sun shall be turned into darkness, And the moon into blood, *before* the coming of the great and awesome day of the LORD' (Joel 2:31; Acts 2:20 KJV). The antichrist must be revealed, the apostasy must occur, the abomination of desolation, lying signs and wonders must occur *before* the coming (*parousia*) of Jesus, the rapture of the church, and the day of Christ (Lord) can come (2 Thess. 2:1-12). Yet, we know that those who hold the testimony of Jesus Christ are not appointed to God's wrath (1 Thess. 1:10; 5:9). So, we know that those in Christ will be removed *before* God's wrath begins.

Remember, the disciples asked what the *sign* of Jesus' *coming* and the *end of the age* (Matt. 24:3) was. We also saw that Jesus said He would be with us (the church - those who hold His testimony) *until* the *end of the age* (Matt. 28:20b). Of course, meaning that the church will remain on earth until the end of the

77

age. And since 1 Thessalonians 4:15-17 says that the church will be caught up together (i.e. raptured) in the air with the Lord; then we must be caught up together (raptured) at the end of the age. So, in light of Scripture, verses 30 and 31 must be referring to the rapture. It fits perfectly in its timing and description, especially when comparing Scripture with Scripture.

Verse 30 NKJV says, 'Then the *sign of the Son of Man will appear in heaven,* and then all the tribes of the earth will mourn, and *they will see the Son of Man coming on the clouds of heaven with power and great glory.*' One might say, 'Wait a minute! Doesn't Christ return like a thief in the night (1 Thess. 5:2)? How can there be a sign at His coming?' I would say that is a very good question. The answer is simple. The day of the Lord (Christ's return) will come as a thief in the night to the ungodly (1 Thess. 5:3), those who are perishing, but not the godly who are looking for the sign of Christ coming and the end of the age. Those in Christ are to remain watchful and sober (1 Thess. 5:4-9). Read the chapter on Thessalonians. You will find a chart in that chapter (chapter 7) comparing Matthew 24:29-31 with 1 Thessalonians 4:13-17.

First we have darkness in the heavens (Matt. 24:29; Mark 13:24-25; Luke 21:25; Rev. 6:12-14), then men will tremble with fear (Matt. 24:29b; Luke 21:26; Rev. 6:15-17), and next Jesus will come in the clouds with great power and glory (Matt. 24:29c; Mark 13:27; Luke 21:27). From great darkness comes great glory and great light. For we who have trusted in Christ as our Lord and Savior, His return is the blessed hope, 'Looking for the blessed hope and glorious appearing of our great God and Savior Jesus Christ' (Titus 2:13 NKJV). From those who are in Christ, Jesus said that He will send His angels with a great sound of a trumpet, and they will *gather together* His elect from the four winds, from one end of heaven to the other (Matt. 24:31). But for those who have rejected Him, His return will be a time of destruction, 'For when *they* say, 'Peace and safety!' then sudden destruction comes upon them, as labor pains upon a pregnant woman. And they shall not escape' (1 Thess. 5:3 NKJV, emphasis added). The previous verse reveals the attitude of the world before God's impending judgment. All the warnings of the coming judgment of God will be ignored. Remember that only the righteous will be persecuted during the great tribulation. The unrighteous will be content and feel no need to be concerned about any future judgment from God. However, at the sign of the day of the Lord (the end of the age), they will tremble with fear (Is. 2:17-19; Joel 2:1-2; Luke 21:25-26; Rev. 6:15-17). Destruction will come as quickly as the sign appears.

Jesus will send His angels to *gather together* His elect. The Greek word for *gather together* is *episunago* (Strong's #1996), which means *to collect upon* to some place. It comes from two Greek words, *epi,* meaning *upon or over* (like the word epidermis - outer or upper layer of skin) and *sunago,* meaning to *collect* (like the word synagogue - assembly or congregation). This gathering is in an upward direction. The direction is of course upward, like the rapture.

I have heard it taught that verse 31 (of Matthew 24) is when Jesus gathers the nation of Israel together to the Holy Mount. However, this cannot be. The Greek language does not allow it. Notice that the elect are gathered *from one end of heaven to the other*. The Greek word for *heaven* is *ouranos* (Strong's #3772), which unmistakably means *sky* or *heaven* (as the abode of God). If Jesus meant a mountain, He would have used the Greek word oros (Strong's #3735), which means a *mountain, hill, or mount.* But this was not the word that Jesus used. He said heaven, which means heaven. Let us compare verse 31 with the other gospels that parallel this verse.

Mark 13:27 KJV says, 'And then shall he send his angels, and shall gather together his elect from the four winds, *from the uttermost (farthest) part of the earth to the uttermost (farthest) part of heaven.*' Notice, '*farthest part of earth to the farthest part of heaven.*' Earth means the ground and heaven means the sky. 1 Thessalonians 4:17, does say that we who are alive and remain (survive) will be caught up together with them (the dead in Christ) and meet the Lord in the air. Those who are alive will come from the earth, their bodies will change into incorruptible bodies at that time (1 Cor. 15:51-53) and the dead in Christ whose spirits/souls are with Christ will return with Him. Since, the dead in Christ have no physical bodies at this time, their spirits/souls are absent from the body, but present with the Lord (2 Cor. 5:8), their bodies will rise first and be changed incorruptible to meet their spirits/souls in the air (1 Cor. 15:51-53). This is why there will be a gathering together 'from the farthest part of earth and the farthest part of heaven.'

In context, speaking of the signs preceding the gathering together (rapture), Luke 21:28 NKJV says, 'Now *when these things begin to happen, look up and lift up your heads, because your redemption draws near*' (emphasis added). Ephesians 4:30 NKJV says, 'And do not grieve the Holy Spirit of God, by whom you were *sealed for the day of redemption.*' (emphasis added) So, if we are sealed until the day of redemption and upon seeing the signs preceding the gathering together, we are told by Jesus to look up because our redemption draws near, then again, this could *only* be the rapture. The rapture occurs at the second coming of Christ. Remember that this is also the end of the age, and after all, there will be a harvest at the end of the age (Matt. 13:39; when the wheat is put into the barn and the tares are burned) and he who endures to the end of the age shall be saved (physically delivered)' (Matt. 24:13). This harvest points to a separation of the righteous and the wicked. The righteous will be rescued and the wicked will be judged. It is Jesus who delivers us from the wrath (God's wrath) to come (1 Thess. 1:10b). Jesus did say in Matthew 28:20b NKJV, in the great commission to the church, 'Lo, I am with you always, *even to the end of the age.*' (emphasis added)

Who Says Matthew 24:29-31 is Not Describing the Rapture?

Many *say* that Matthew 24:29-31 is referring to the Battle of Armageddon. Therefore, I have included a chart which compares Revelation 19:11-16, the Armageddon passage, with Matthew 24:29-31 and 1 Thessalonians 4:13-17 (the rapture passage). As always, we will compare Scripture with Scripture. You can read the following three passages of Scripture and then compare them on the chart that follows.

1 Thessalonians 4:13-17 KJV

[13] 'But I would not have you to be ignorant, brethren, concerning them which are asleep, that ye sorrow not, even as others which have no hope. [14]For if we believe that Jesus died and rose again, even so them also which sleep in Jesus will God bring with him. [15]For this we say unto you by the word of the Lord, that we which are alive *and* remain unto the coming of the Lord shall not prevent them which are asleep. [16]For the Lord himself shall descend from heaven with a shout, with the voice of the archangel, and with the trump of God: and the dead in Christ shall rise first: [17]Then we which are alive *and* remain shall be caught up together with them in the clouds, to meet the Lord in the air: and so shall we ever be with the Lord.'

Revelation 19:11-21 KJV

[11] 'And I saw heaven opened, and behold a white horse; and he that sat upon him *was* called Faithful and True, and in righteousness he doth judge and make war. [12]His eyes *were* as a flame of fire, and on his head *were* many crowns; and he had a name written, that no man knew, but he himself. [13]And he *was* clothed with a vesture dipped in blood: and his name is called The Word of God. [14]And the armies *which were* in heaven followed him upon white horses, clothed in fine linen, white and clean. [15]And out of his mouth goeth a sharp sword, that with it he should smite the nations: and he shall rule them with a rod of iron: and he treadeth the winepress of the fierceness and wrath of Almighty God. [16]And he hath on *his* vesture and on his thigh a name written, KING OF KINGS, AND LORD OF LORDS. [17]And I saw an angel standing in the sun; and he cried with a loud voice, saying to all the fowls that fly in the midst of heaven, Come and gather yourselves together unto the supper of the great God; [18]That ye may eat the flesh of kings, and the flesh of captains, and the flesh of mighty men, and the flesh of horses, and of them that sit on them, and the flesh of all *men, both* free and bond, both

small and great. [19]And I saw the beast, and the kings of the earth, and their armies, gathered together to make war against him that sat on the horse, and against his army. [20]And the beast was taken, and with him the false prophet that wrought miracles before him, with which he deceived them that had received the mark of the beast, and them that worshipped his image. These both were cast alive into a lake of fire burning with brimstone. [21]And the remnant were slain with the sword of him that sat upon the horse, which *sword* proceeded out of his mouth: and all the fowls were filled with their flesh.'

Matthew 24:29-31 KJV

[29]'Immediately after the tribulation of those days shall the sun be darkened, and the moon shall not give her light, and the stars shall fall from heaven, and the powers of the heavens shall be shaken: [30]And then shall appear the sign of the Son of man in heaven: and then shall all the tribes of the earth mourn, and they shall see the Son of man coming in the clouds of heaven with power and great glory. [31]And he shall send his angels with a great sound of a trumpet, and they shall gather together his elect from the four winds, from one end of heaven to the other.'

COMPARING SCRIPTURE WITH SCRIPTURE

Matthew 24:29-31 parallels 1 Thessalonians 4:13-17 (the Rapture Passage) - NOT Revelation 19:11-21 (the Armageddon Passage)

"See for yourself"

1 THESSALONIANS 4:13-17	REVELATION 19:11-21	MATTHEW 24:29-31
V 16 THE LORD DESCENDS FROM HEAVEN	CHRIST SEEN IN HEAVEN Verses 11-13	SON OF MAN APPEARS IN HEAVEN V 30
V 16 TRUMPET OF GOD	*Has No Comparison*	GREAT SOUND OF A TRUMPET V 31
V 16 VOICE OF ARCHANGEL	*Has No Comparison*	HE SENDS HIS ANGELS V 31
V 17 CAUGHT UP TOGETHER (BELIEVERS)	*Has No Comparison*	GATHER TOGETHER HIS ELECT V 31
V 17 MEET THEM IN THE CLOUDS	*Has No Comparison*	SON OF MAN IN THE CLOUDS V 30

After comparing the three previous Scriptures, it could only be concluded that Matthew 24: 29-31 is closely related to 1 Thessalonians 4:13-17 (the rapture passage). Revelation 19:11-16 literally has no comparison to the other two passages and cannot legitimately be referring to the same event.

The Parable of the Fig Tree

[32] 'Now learn a parable of the fig tree; When his branch is yet tender, and putteth forth leaves, ye know that summer *is* nigh: [33]So likewise ye, when ye shall see all these things, know that it is near, *even* at the doors. [34]Verily I say unto you, This generation shall not pass, till all these things be fulfilled. [35]Heaven and earth shall pass away, but my words shall not pass away.' (Matt. 24:32-35 KJV)

Verses 4 through 31 of Matthew 24 literally complete the answer to the questions that the disciples privately asked Jesus on the Mount Olives. Remember that they asked Jesus what will be the sign of His coming *(parousia)* and the end of the age (v3)? Jesus tells them to be watchful and look for the signs. Signs are visible things. First, He tells them the simple parable of the fig tree. (We might call it a metaphor or an analogy.)

The Greek word for *parable* is *parabole* (Strong's #3580), which means *a placing beside*. It comes from two Greek words: *Para*, which means *alongside* (like our word parallel) and *ballo*, which means to *cast or throw* (like throwing a ball). So, it is when an earthly story that should be easy to understand is placed alongside something being taught in order to give a more meaningful understanding of what is being taught.

Many are misled when they take this parable that should be seen as a simple analogy, and view it as an allegory. An allegory is when you take something that is meant to mean one thing and make it a symbolic representation of something else, thereby missing what is truly being taught. This is somewhat common. If we take it upon ourselves to allegorize Scripture, we can make it say almost anything we want it to say, which causes confusion. However, having said that, Jesus does give *the signs of His return.* These are very specific signs that will occur in the last days (in Israel especially, but also throughout the world) that show we will have less than 3 ½ years until His return. The generation living when these signs occur, will see the return of our Lord and Savior Jesus Christ.

Some take this parable to mean that the fig tree is the nation of Israel. Since Israel became a nation again in 1948, and is now back in the land, they say that the leaves on the fig tree are now budding and Christ will return in this generation (however many years one might consider a generation to be). I believe that there are many problems with that interpretation. I will explain, but it is very important to understand the context in which this statement was made.

When Jesus told them to *learn* this parable, He used the Greek word *manthano*, (Strong's #3129), which means *to learn by inquiry or observation,* also it literally means *to learn by practicing as a habit in life.* In Philippians 4:11, Paul said that he had *learned* to be content whatever the circumstances. This is the same Greek word from Matthew. Jesus was not only speaking to the disciples, but also to the generation living during the time all these things would happen. He uses the word *you* in verses 4, 6, 9, 15, 23, and 25.

Jesus never said that the fig tree was Israel. In taking it upon ourselves to do this, we make an allegory out of something that was meant to be used as a simple analogy. There were many fig trees in Israel. The disciples knew from their childhood that they could tell that summer was near by looking at the leaves budding on the many fig trees. I am from South Georgia where there are many pecan trees. Even as a child, I knew that when the leaves and pecans fell (October/November), it was pecan season. The temperature got cooler, and it was time for the Fair to come to town. Just as I learned from childhood what to expect when the leaves fell from the pecan trees, the disciples understood what Jesus' parable of the fig tree meant. It simply meant to look around and pay attention. All these things will happen before He returns.

The generation that sees all the things that He just told them about will not pass away before He returns.

The Day and Hour, No One Knows

> [36] 'But of that day and hour knoweth no man, no, not the angels of heaven, but my Father only. [37]But as the days of Noe (Noah) were, so shall also the coming of the Son of man be. [38]For as in the days that were before the flood they were eating and drinking, marrying and giving in marriage, until the day that Noe (Noah) entered into the ark, [39]And knew not until the flood came, and *took* them all away; so shall also the coming of the Son of man be. [40]Then shall two be in the field; the one shall be *taken*, and the other *left*. [41]Two women shall be grinding at the mill; the one shall be *taken*, and the other *left*. [42]*Watch* therefore: for ye know not what hour your Lord doth come. [43]But know this, that if the goodman of the house had known in what watch the thief would come, he would have watched, and would not have suffered his house to be broken up. [44]Therefore be ye also ready: for in such an hour as ye think not the Son of man cometh.' (Matthew 24:36-44 KJV, emphasis added)

I have heard what I consider very good Bible teachers, teach verses 37 through 42 and come to a different conclusion than what the Greek is actually saying in these verses. This is probably because most teach it from the pre-tribulation view. If you hold or have held that view, you probably believe that the verse referring to the taking away of the men in the field and the women grinding refers to them being taken to judgment and the ones left will go into the millennial kingdom.

Verses 37 and 38 compare the days of Noah (just before the flood) with the days just before the coming (*parousia*) of Christ. When it says that the people in Noah's time were eating, drinking, marrying, and giving in marriage until the day that Noah entered the ark (v 38), it is not referring to anything necessarily sinful about their lives (even though their lives were), but that they had no idea about the judgment to come. It will be the same way before the coming of Christ. They will be unaware of the judgment from God to come. Verse 39 KJV says, 'And knew not until the flood came, and *took* them all away; so shall also the coming of the Son of man be.' The Greek word for *took* here is *airo* (Strong's #142), which means *to take up or away* or *remove*. They were obviously taken away to judgment. It will also be the same way at the coming of Christ. It is important that we understand a couple of Greek words in the next few verses and compare them with the Greek word *airo*.

Verse 40 and 41 KJV says, 'Then shall two be in the field; the one shall be *taken*, and the other *left*. Two women shall be grinding at the mill; the one shall be *taken*, and the other *left*.' Most will assume that the word *took* in verse 39 is the same as the word *taken* in verses 41 and 42, assuming that they are being taken to judgment. However, that is not the case. The Greek word for *taken* in verses 41 and 42 is *paralambano* (Strong's #3880), which means *to receive near* or to *associate with* oneself (in a familiar or intimate act or relation). It literally means to *receive alongside*. Clearly, the ones being taken in verses 40 and 41 are *not* taken to judgment, but are received alongside Christ (the one doing the taking). This is another view of how the rapture will be at Christ's second coming.

Many view John 14:1-3 KJV as a rapture passage. It reads, 'Let not your heart be troubled: ye believe in God, believe also in me. In my Father's house are many mansions: if *it were* not *so*, I would have told you. I go to prepare a place for you. And if I go and prepare a place for you, *I will come again, and receive you unto myself;* that where I am, *there* ye may be also' (emphasis added).

Notice that Jesus said, 'I will come again and *receive* you unto Myself.' The Greek word for *receive* is *paralambano*. This is of course the same word as *taken* in a previous paragraph. It is an endearing term. So it should be clear that those being taken are received alongside Christ in verse 41 and 42. But, what about those who are *left*? If the ones being taken are with Christ, then the others who are left should be *left* for judgment. The Greek word used for *left* is *aphiemi* (Strong's #863), which means to *send forth, leave, lay aside, omit, remit, suffer;* basically it means here *to leave one by not taking him as a companion.*

Now, with what you have learned about what the Greek is actually saying, would you want to be the one *taken* alongside Christ or the one *left* to suffer without Christ as a companion. The answer should be simple. I would rather be the one taken alongside Christ. The ones *left* on earth are *left* to experience God's wrath during the day of the Lord.

Jesus has been talking about signs, which means that there is something to watch out for. The last warning that we will cover is in verse 42. In lieu of all the things that Jesus has said, He says, '*Watch* therefore,' because we do not know that hour of His coming. The Greek word is *gregoreuo* (Strong's #1127), which means to *keep awake, be vigilant, be watchful.* Yes, we are to be watchful (verses 36-44). The parable of the Faithful and Evil Servant (Matt. 24:45-51) reminds us to be *faithful* servants of Christ until His Return. The parable of the Wise and Foolish Virgins reminds us to be *prepared* for Christ's Return (Matt. 25:1-13), and the parable of the Talents reminds us to be *fruitful* (Matt. 25:14-30) with what we have received until our Lord and Savior's coming (*parousia*).

Learn from the Days of Noah and Lot

There is one other important thing to learn from Noah's day. On the very same day that Noah and his family entered the ark, judgment began on earth (Gen. 7:11-13). Jesus made this comparison in Luke 17.

> ²⁶ 'And as it was in the days of Noe (Noah), so shall it be also in the days of the Son of man. ²⁷They did eat, they drank, they married wives, they were given in marriage, *until the day* that Noe (Noah) entered into the ark, and the flood came, and destroyed them all. ²⁸Likewise also as it was in the days of Lot; they did eat, they drank, they

bought, they sold, they planted, they builded; [29]But *the same day* that Lot went out of Sodom it rained fire and brimstone from heaven, and destroyed them all. [30]Even thus shall it be *in the day* when the Son of man is revealed.' (Luke 17:26-30 KJV, emphasis added)

We find that on the very day that the righteous ones were delivered, the unrighteous are judged. Could this mean that the rapture occurs on the very day that the day of the LORD begins? Yes, it does. Jesus made a clear comparison. 'On the day' that Noah and Lot where rescued, the wicked were destroyed. It will happen the same way when Jesus is revealed at His coming. Being that these are the two historical events compared in the gospels to the day of the LORD, what can we tell from them? (1) In both cases, God rescues the godly from His coming judgment. (2) The ungodly were punished/destroyed during His judgment. (3) Judgment came suddenly, on the very same day as the rescue. (4) Both Noah and Lot were warned of the coming judgment.

The return of Christ will be a time of great joy for those in Christ, but a time of destruction for those who are left. Yes, on the very same day of the rapture will come the day of the Lord (God's wrath upon the ungodly).

Chapter 7

Thessalonians – The Words of Paul

There is much to learn about the coming of Christ and the sequence of events surrounding His return in the two letters written to the Thessalonians. The general sequence of events is (1) the tribulation or persecution of the righteous (believers), (2) the deliverance (the rescue or removal) of the righteous (before the day of the Lord) and (3) then the judgment of the ungodly during the day of the Lord. So, we will find persecution of the believers, deliverance of believers, and then God's wrath upon the ungodly. This sequence of events is repeated over and over again in the Bible. We will also find this in Paul's letter to the Thessalonians.

Paul obviously taught the believers in Thessalonica about the return of Christ (the day of the Lord – 1 Thess. 5:2). They were deeply concerned about the believers who died since Paul taught them about Christ's return. Paul did not want them to be uninformed about what would happen to those who died believing in Christ, so he addressed this issue in his first letter to them. His wrote the following:

[13] 'But I would not have you to be ignorant, brethren, concerning them which are asleep, that ye sorrow not, even

as others which have no hope. [14]For if we believe that Jesus died and rose again, even so *them also which sleep in Jesus will God bring with him.* [15]For this we say unto you by the word of the Lord, that *we which are alive and remain unto the coming of the Lord* shall not prevent them which are asleep. [16]For the Lord himself shall descend from heaven with a shout, with the voice of the archangel, and with the trump of God: and the dead in Christ shall rise first: [17]Then we which are alive and remain shall be caught up together with them in the clouds, to meet the Lord in the air: and so shall we ever be with the Lord. [18]Wherefore comfort one another with these words.' (1 Thess. 4:13-18 KJV, emphasis added)

Verses 13 - 15

Paul said that he did not want them to be ignorant about those who had died (fallen asleep in Christ). He said this because they were ignorant about it. In verse 13, Paul did not want them to be sorrowful as those who have no hope. Those who have no hope are the unsaved. He lets them know that at the return of Christ, the believers who have died in Christ would be brought back with Jesus. They would see their fellow believers at this time. Keep in mind that all who have died in Christ *are absent from the body, but present with the Lord* (2 Corinthians 5:8). For Christians, at death, it is the physical body that sleeps (in the grave), but the soul goes on to be with the Lord. However, the body and the soul will be reunited at the rapture. Just as Jesus died and rose from the grave with a glorified body, so will the souls of those who died in Christ come back with Jesus. Their bodies will rise from the grave and meet their souls. They will receive their glorified bodies at that time.

It is obvious that this teaching personally came from Jesus (v 15); however, what is not clear is whether Paul received this from a direct revelation from Christ (1 Cor. 11:23) or was it what Christ taught the disciples concerning His return (Matt. 24:29-31; Mark

13:24-27; Luke 21:25-28)? Actually, it really does not matter, because Christ's teaching will not contradict itself. So in context, it should parallel and be harmonized elsewhere in Scripture.

Paul said in verse 15, '...*we which are alive and remain unto (until) the coming of the Lord* shall not prevent them which are asleep.' The word *we*, of course speaks of believers in Christ. Believers will remain on earth until Christ's coming (*parousia* - Strong's #3952, meaning a *presence, a presence with*). The text says, not only *we who will be alive*, but also *we who remain.* The Greek word used here for *remain* is *perileipo* (Strong's #4035), which literally means to *survive* (or *leave around*). It is only used twice in the New Testament; once here and again in verse 17. The logical question is what would they have to survive? The logical answer would be persecution and tribulation (1 Thess. 2:14; 2 Thess. 1:4). Jesus clearly taught that there would be persecution of the elect before His return (Matt. 24:4-25). This was also the teaching of Paul (as was John in the book of Revelation). The believers who survive until the coming (*parousia*) of Christ 'will by no means precede those who are asleep' (1 Thess. 4:15b NKJV). In the Greek, this statement '*by no means*' has a double negative to assure without a doubt that they should not worry about those who died in Christ. The living survivors will not go *before* the dead in Christ.

It is important to note here that the coming (*parousia*) of Jesus Christ is closely associated with the rapture of the church and not a separate event. We saw this in the previous chapters on Matthew 24 (Chapter 6) and the Coming of Christ (Chapter 5). Contrary to what other views teach, there are signs associated with the rapture, which will be visible. The rapture will not be a secret event. The disciples asked Jesus about the *sign* associated with His coming (*parousia*) and the end of the age (Matt. 24:3-31; Mark 13:3-27).

Verses 16 - 18

We find that Jesus will descend from heaven. 'For the Lord Himself (Jesus) will descend from heaven with a shout, with the voice of an archangel, and with the trumpet of God. And the dead in Christ will rise first' (v 16). The *Interlinear Greek English New Testament* says, 'The literal translation of the Greek would read, 'Because the Lord Himself shall come down from Heaven with a trumpet-call of an archangel's voice, and with God's trumpet. And the dead in Christ will rise again first.'' [1]

After the dead in Christ rise, the believers who survive until the coming (*parousia*) of Christ will be *caught up* together to meet the Lord in the air. The Greek word for *caught up* is *harpazo* (Strong's #726), which means to *seize, snatch or catch away*. (Although the word *rapture* is not found in Scripture, this event is clearly taught. The English word 'rapture' comes directly from the Latin word *raptus*, meaning a *carrying or taking away.* The stated outcome of this is that we will always be with the Lord.

The Thessalonians are told to comfort each other with those words (v18). These words must have comforted the believers in Paul's day, as they should also comfort believers in our day. In a three-year period, I lost my brother, father, and then my mother. My confidence in Paul's words gave me strength during those tough times as they still do today. I look forward to the return of Christ and also to a reunion in the clouds with my loved ones who have gone on before me.

Christ's coming (*parousia*) in 1 Thessalonians 4:13-17 should be compared with Matt. 24:29-31; Mark 13:24-27; and Luke 21:25-28. In comparing Scripture surrounding the coming (*parousia*) of Christ, note *Christ's descent, the archangel's (angels) involvement, the trumpet of God, the clouds,* and *the gathering together*. Also, note that they are all in the context of Christ's return. This means that we can learn more about this event by comparing each passage with the other. I have provided a chart comparing 1 Thessalonians 4:13-17 and Matthew 24:29-31.

COMPARING SCRIPTURE WITH SCRIPTURE

The Rapture Passage in 1 Thessalonians 4 and the Coming (*Parousia*) of Christ in Matthew 24

1 THESSALONIANS 4:13-17		MATTHEW 24:29-31	
V 16	THE LORD DESCENDS FROM HEAVEN	V 30	SON OF MAN APPEARS IN HEAVEN
V 16	TRUMPET OF GOD	V 31	GREAT SOUND OF A TRUMPET
V 16	VOICE OF ARCHANGEL	V 31	HE SENDS HIS ANGELS
V 17	CAUGHT UP TOGETHER (BELIEVERS)	V 31	GATHER TOGETHER HIS ELECT
V 17	MEET THEM IN THE CLOUDS	V 30	SON OF MAN IN THE CLOUDS

It can be clearly seen that the coming (*parousia*) of Christ described in the Olivet Discourse from Matthew 24:29-31 is the same event described in 1 Thessalonians 4:13-17. This event is of course the rapture of the true church/elect. However, some (the pre-tribulationalists) believe that the compared events mentioned above in the gospels (Matthew 24; Mark 13; and Luke 21) are not talking about the rapture of the church, but the Battle of Armageddon. Pre-tribulationists must teach this because they believe the church is removed before the tribulation begins. Comparing Revelation 19:11-21 (the Battle of Armageddon passage) with the above Scriptures will prove otherwise. A more complete comparison (along with a chart) was given in the latter part of chapter 6 of this book (the chapter on Matthew 24). The comparison will reveal that it simply cannot be the same event described in Matthew 24 and 1 Thessalonians 4. The events mentioned in the gospels (Matt. 24:29-31; Mark 13:24-27; and Luke 21:25-28) could only be describing the rapture. Another interesting point to note is that in the context of the end times, Jesus said in Matthew 24:13 and Mark 13:13 that he who endures (the persecution) until the end (the end of the age/Christ's coming) shall be saved (delivered physically).

1 Thessalonians 5 – The Day of the Lord

After Paul instructs the Thessalonians about the subject of the dead in Christ and the rapture of the believers, he continues about the day of the Lord. It should be noted that so far as the subject of the dead in Christ was concerned, the Thessalonians were ignorant of the subject. However, as far as the subject of the day of the Lord was concerned, the Thessalonians had a complete knowledge of the times and the seasons. It should also be noted that Paul's letter was not originally divided into chapters and verses. So, do not let this chapter division throw you off. Chapter 5 verse 1 is a continuation of the thought and subject (rapture) discussed in the latter part of chapter 4. Paul's words read as follows.

> [1] 'But of the times and the seasons, brethren, ye have no need that I write unto you. [2]For yourselves know perfectly that the day of the Lord so cometh as a thief in the night. [3]For when they shall say, Peace and safety; then sudden destruction cometh upon them, as travail upon a woman with child; and they shall not escape. [4]But ye, brethren, are not in darkness, that that day should overtake you as a thief. [5]Ye are all the children of light, and the children of the day: we are not of the night, nor of darkness. [6]Therefore let us not sleep, as *do* others; but let us watch and be sober. [7]For they that sleep sleep in the night; and they that be drunken are drunken in the night. [8]But let us, who are of the day, be sober, putting on the breastplate of faith and love; and for an helmet, the hope of salvation. [9]For God hath not appointed us to wrath, but to obtain salvation by our Lord Jesus Christ, [10]Who died for us, that, whether we wake or sleep, we should live together with him. [11]Wherefore comfort yourselves together, and edify one another, even as also ye do.' (1 Thess. 5:1-11 KJV)

Verses 1 - 6

Even though the Thessalonians lacked understanding of the

dead in Christ at Jesus' return, they had a perfect understanding of the times and the seasons of the day of the Lord. 'The day of the Lord so comes as a thief in the night,' to the unbelievers (v 2, NKJV). Notice the third person plural (they, them) in verse 3. 'When *they* say, 'Peace and safety!' then sudden destruction will come upon *them* and *they* will not escape (v 3 NKJV).' God's wrath and the destruction of the ungodly are closely associated with the day of the Lord. The use of *they* and *them* obviously point away from the believers to *the ungodly.* Keep in mind that the ungodly are not being persecuted during the great tribulation. Only those who do not follow the antichrist or take his mark are persecuted.

Paul next shifts to the second and first person plural (you, we) in verses 4-6. Although the day of the Lord will come as a thief in the night to the ungodly, it will *not* come as a surprise to the watchful believers. To the believers, Paul says, 'But *you*, brethren, are not in darkness, so that this Day (the day of the Lord) would overtake *you* as a thief. *You* are all sons of light and sons of the day. *We* are not of the night, nor of darkness. *Therefore* let *us* not sleep, as *others* do, but let *us* watch and be sober' (verses 4-6, NKJV). In other words, we are of the day, living in the light and have been warned what is to come. Signs of the day of the Lord (the coming of Christ) are clearly given. Let us pay attention to our surroundings and not sleep as the *others (the ungodly)* do.

Verses 7 - 8

Verses 7 and 8 expound further on verse 6, '*For those who sleep, sleep at night, and those who get drunk are drunk at night. But let us who are of the day be sober, putting on the breastplate of faith and love, and as a helmet the hope of salvation.*' Those of the ungodly world are not only asleep, but are drunk as well. They are not only asleep in darkness, but are drunk with the lusts of the world and what it has to offer. They have no idea of what is to come or the timing thereof. The world at the coming (*parousia*) of Christ will be as the world was in the days of Noah, not having any idea of the judgment that was about to come (Matt. 24:36-44). But *we* who are living in the day should remain sober. We should put on faith and love (v 8). We should look for our future *salvation.* The Greek word for *salvation* is *soteria* (Strong's #4991), which means *rescue, deliverance* (it can be spiritual and or physical deliverance). Although we are spiritually saved, there is a promise of physical deliverance to the faithful believers who endure the persecution to the end of the age/the day of the Lord (Matt. 13:13; Matt. 24:13).

Not Appointed to God's Wrath

'For God hath not appointed us to wrath, but to obtain salvation by our Lord Jesus Christ (v 9).' Believers will be physically delivered from the wrath to come (1 Thess. 1:10). Remember our sequence mentioned earlier in the chapter, *first* tribulation/persecution of the righteous (this persecution comes from the ungodly, led by the antichrist), *next* physical deliverance (*soteria*) through rapture, and *then* the wrath of God upon the ungodly on earth. Believers are not appointed to God's wrath; however, the church will have to endure the wrath of Satan (during the great tribulation). Scripture is extremely clear about the separation of God's wrath and Satan's wrath. These two events cannot possibly be the same. We saw this in chapter 4, the chapter dealing with God's wrath (the day of the Lord) and Satan's wrath (the great tribulation).

Jesus endured the wrath of God while on the cross in our behalf; therefore, we who are in Christ are not appointed to God's wrath. Paul comforts the Thessalonians assuring them that even though they would have to endure persecution and tribulation from man, as they were enduring (1 Thess. 2:14; 2 Thess.1: 4), they would be delivered (saved) from God's wrath that was yet future. The pre-tribulation argument uses Revelation 3:10 as a proof text for the removal of the church from the earth *before* the worldwide tribulation from the antichrist begins. Read the chapter on Revelation 3:10 (Chapter 8). It will give you insight on the Greek text and its true meaning.

Looking Forward to the Blessed Hope

It is obvious that in verse 10 Paul tells the Thessalonians who were concerned about those who slept (died in Christ), 'Whether *we wake* (alive at the coming of Christ) or *sleep* (dead in Christ), *we should live together with Him*' (v 10). This verse further ties the rapture (1 Thess. 4:13-17) to the day of the Lord (1 Thess. 5:1-9). They are also told a second time to comfort each other (1 Thess. 4:18; 5:11).

Concerning the coming (*parousia*) of Christ, we should be *watchful*, just as Jesus taught the disciples at the Olivet Discourse. We should look for *signs* around us (as in the parable of the fig tree, Matt. 24:32-35), be *faithful* (as in the parable of the faithful and evil servant, Matt. 24:45-51), be *prepared* (as the five wise virgins in the parable of the ten virgins, Matt. 25:1-13), and be *fruitful* (as in the parable of the talents, Matt. 25:14-30).

We have a blessed hope in the future appearing of our Lord and Savior Jesus Christ (Titus 2:13). In the book of Titus, we receive instructions on how to live until the coming of Jesus.

[11] 'For the grace of God that bringeth salvation hath appeared to all men, [12]Teaching us that, *denying ungodliness and worldly lusts, we should live soberly, righteously, and godly, in this present world;* [13]*Looking for that blessed hope, and the glorious appearing of the great God and our Saviour Jesus Christ;* [14]Who gave himself for us, that he might redeem us from all iniquity, and purify unto himself a peculiar people, zealous of good works.' (Titus 2:11-14 KJV, emphasis added)

It is clear that in Titus, Paul's words are encouraging believers to deny the ungodly and worldly lusts and live sober, righteous, and godly lives. Some think that it would not be a blessed hope, if we experience the tribulation; think again. The Scriptures say,

'That no one should be shaken by these afflictions; for you yourselves know that we are appointed to this. For, in fact, we told you before when we were with you that *we would suffer tribulation,* just as it happened, and you know' (1 Thessalonians 3:3-4 NKJV, emphasis added).

> [10] 'Blessed are those who are persecuted for righteousness' sake, For theirs is the kingdom of heaven. [11]Blessed are you when they revile and persecute you, and say all kinds of evil against you falsely for My sake. [12]Rejoice and be exceedingly glad, for great *is* your reward in heaven, for so they persecuted the prophets who were before you.' (Matt. 5:10-12 NKJV)

'Yes, and all who desire to live godly in Christ will suffer persecution' (1 Timothy 3:12 NKJV). No matter what comes, our eyes should be focused on Christ. Our blessed hope is that whether we are alive or dead, we in Christ will not miss His glorious appearance.

2 Thessalonians 1

As we saw in first Thessalonians, Paul again addressed the concerns about what would happen to those who had died in Christ. The Thessalonians had been taught that they were *not* appointed to God's wrath (1 Thess. 5:9); which begins at the day of the Lord and would be delivered from the wrath to come (1 Thess. 1:10). However, shortly after the first letter to the Thessalonians was written, another problem had risen in Thessalonica. They somehow were told that the day of the Lord had come and that they were experiencing God's wrath. This of course would mean that they had missed the rapture, which could not be. Whether they had received a letter from someone claiming to be Paul or by the word of a false prophet is not clear. The fact of the matter is that there was misunderstanding and confusion about the events surrounding the day of the Lord. Paul further addressed this issue about the gathering together (the rapture) and the day of the Lord in the second letter to the Thessalonians (2 Thessalonians. 2:1).

> [3] 'We are bound to thank God always for you, brethren, as it is meet, because that *your faith groweth exceedingly, and the charity (love) of every one of you all toward each other aboundeth;* [4]So that we ourselves glory in you in the churches of God for *your patience and faith in all your persecutions and tribulations that ye endure:* [5]Which is a manifest token of the righteous judgment of God, that ye may be counted worthy of the kingdom of God, for which ye also suffer: [6]*Seeing it is a righteous thing with God to recompense tribulation to them that trouble you;* [7]*And to you who are troubled rest with us, when the Lord Jesus shall be revealed from heaven with his mighty angels,* [8]*In flaming fire taking vengeance on them that know not God, and that obey not the gospel of our Lord Jesus Christ:* [9]Who shall be punished with everlasting destruction from the presence of the Lord, and from the glory of his power; [10]When he shall come to be glorified in his saints, and to be admired in all them that believe (because our testimony among you was believed) in that day.' (2 Thess. 1:3-10 KJV, emphasis added)

Paul had previously told the church in Thessalonica to put on faith and love as they looked for the return of Christ (1 Thess. 5:8). He thanked the Lord because their faith and love was growing exceedingly (2 Thess. 2:3).

Again, we will see a sequence of events that repeat over and over in Scripture, (*tribulation, persecution of righteous, deliverance of the righteous, and then judgment of the ungodly*). In verses 4 through 10, we see precisely that. They were patient and faithful in all of the 'persecution and tribulation' that they continued to endure (v 4) which was evident of the righteous judgment of God.' (v 5) They were suffering for the kingdom of God. The *next* thing we find is that God will *repay* with tribulation those who trouble them (v 6) and give *rest* to those who are troubled (the righteous, those in Christ). When? Paul tells them that this will happen at the coming (*parousia*) of Christ, *when* the Lord Jesus is revealed from heaven with his mighty angels (v 7). God's vengeance will be taken 'out on those who do not know God and on those who do not obey the gospel of our Lord Jesus Christ.' (v 8)

Vengeance is the Lord's - God will repay

Verses 6 through 8 describe how God will repay with tribulation those who were persecuting His servants. God will avenge the blood of His own. Vengeance does not belong to us. It belongs to God alone. Scripture says, "*Vengeance is Mine, I will repay,*' says the Lord' (Deut. 32:35; Heb. 10:30; Rom. 12:19). This is the principle of divine retribution (*lex talionis* (an eye for an eye, a tooth for a tooth).

The Christians in Rome received this instruction from Paul, '*Repay no one evil for evil.* Have regard for good things in the sight of all men. If it is possible, as much as depends on you, live peaceably with all men. Beloved, *do not avenge yourselves, but rather give place to wrath:* for it is written, '*Vengeance is Mine, I will repay,*' says the Lord' (Rom. 12:17-19 NKJV, emphasis added).

The persecuted saints (true Christians) in the book of Revelation are also encouraged to remain faithful; whether imprisoned or killed, because God will repay those who trouble His own. 'He who leads into captivity shall go into captivity; he who kills with the sword must be killed with the sword. *Here is the patience and the faith of the saints*' (Rev. 13:10 NKJV, emphasis added).

Again, Jesus said in context on His coming, '*But he who endures to the end shall be saved (physical deliverance, raptured)*' (Matthew 24:13; Mark 13:13b NKJV, emphasis added). This obviously coincides with what the faithful saints in Thessalonica were told by Paul.

Eternal Punishment for the Ungodly

In 2 Thessalonians 1:9-10, we find that the price for the ungodly world to pay is 'everlasting destruction from the presence of God.' When? '*When His comes, in that Day* (day of the Lord), to be *glorified in His saints* and to be admired among all those who believe, because our testimony among you was believed.' We are to have faith in God's word and remain patient while enduring persecution, because God will avenge the blood of His own in His own time.

2 Thessalonians 2

We just saw in chapter one of 2 Thessalonians that Paul commended the Thessalonians for their patience and love while suffering persecution and assured them that God would give them relief. The Lord would *repay* those who persecuted them with His divine judgment. They knew that tribulation would come *before* the rapture and that God's wrath would come upon the ungodly afterwards. Yet, they needed more clarification about the timing of the day of the Lord.

We now move on to the second chapter of second Thessalonians. Here we see that Paul explains why it is impossible for the day of the Lord to have already arrived. These verses will provide specific events that will occur *before* the coming (*pauousia*) of Christ, our gathering together (*rapture*), and the day of the Lord (*God's wrath*). It also quite clearly ties these three events together. If you read the following verses in its most natural sense (without preconceived ideas), you will find Paul made things unmistakably clear. After all, this was his purpose for writing. Harmonizing the following Scriptures with the gospels, with Daniel, and with Revelation will provide great insight on the end times surrounding the coming of Christ. A chart (End Times Chart – Harmonizing Scripture) is provided to assist you in comparing Scripture and to deepen your understanding. 2 Thessalonians, verses 1-12 read as follows:

¹ 'Now we beseech you, brethren, by the *coming of our Lord Jesus Christ, and by our gathering together unto him,* ²That ye be not soon shaken in mind, or be troubled, neither by spirit, nor by word, nor by letter as from us, as that the day of Christ is at hand. ³Let no man deceive you by any means: for that day shall not come, except there come a falling away first, and that man of sin be revealed, the son of perdition; ⁴Who opposeth and exalteth himself above all that is called God, or that is worshipped; so that he as God sitteth in the temple of God, showing himself that he is God. ⁵Remember ye not, that, when I was yet with you, I told you these things? ⁶And now ye know what withholdeth that he might be revealed in his time. ⁷For the mystery of iniquity doth already work: only he who now letteth will let, until he be taken out of the way. ⁸And then shall that Wicked be revealed, whom the Lord shall consume with the spirit of his mouth, and shall destroy with the brightness of his coming: ⁹*Even him,* whose coming is after the working of Satan with all power and signs and lying wonders, ¹⁰And with all deceivableness of unrighteousness in them that perish; because they received not the love of the truth, that they might be saved. ¹¹And for this cause God shall send them strong delusion, that they should believe a lie: ¹²That they all might be damned who believed not the truth, but had pleasure in unrighteousness.' (2 Thess. 2:1-12 KJV, emphasis added)

The subject matter is clear. It is 'concerning the coming (*parousia*) of our Lord Jesus Christ and our gathering together to Him (v 1).' The disciples asked Jesus for the sign of *His coming* (*parousia*) (Matt. 24:3). Jesus gave a specific sign (Matt. 24:29-30) and the immediate timing associated with *His coming* and *our gathering together* (Matt. 24:31). We saw the same event discussed in 1 Thessalonians 4:16-17 (the rapture). According to Jesus, these events will occur immediately after the tribulation. You may say, does not the tribulation period last seven years? The short answer to that question would be, 'No.' What lasts seven years is the 70th week of Daniel (Dan. 9:27). The tribulation or great tribulation (a time of persecution of the elect, saints, bondservants, and/or true church) occurs within the 70th week of Daniel and will be 'cut short' for the sake of the elect (Matt. 24:22). The tribulation does not run to the end of the 70th week of Daniel. The ones who survive to the end of this tribulation period will be alive and delivered at the rapture (Matt. 24:13), our gathering together (2 Thess. 2:1). Read the chapter on Matthew 24 for more detail on this subject.

In verse 2, Paul immediately clears the air by letting them know that there is no need to be disturbed or troubled in their mind or spirit, thinking that the day of Christ (the Lord) had come. It had not. After making it clear that the day of the Lord had not come, Paul moves on to events that must occur *before* that Day (the day of the Lord) can come.

The Apostasy

Paul begins verse 3 by saying to them, 'Let no one deceive you by any means.' Why? Because the day of the Lord cannot come unless, '*the falling away comes first,* and the *man of sin is revealed, the son of perdition.*' The Greek word for *falling away* is *apostasia* (Strong's # 646); it means a *defection or revolt,* a literal *defection from the truth,* apostasy. (You will find this word used twice in the New Testament, here and in Acts 21:21). In the Greek text, the word has a definite article (the) before it. This means that it refers to a specific future falling away (apostasy) associated with the revealing of this man of sin, the son of perdition (the antichrist). So the antichrist who will be revealed and the apostasy both occur *before* the rapture.

In the context of this same time, Matthew 24:10 NKJV says, 'And then many will be *offended,* will betray one another, and will hate one another.' The Greek word for *offended* is *skandalizo* (Strong's #4624), which means to *entrap or entice to sin, apostasy or displeasure; to make to offend.* Literally, it means to cause a person to begin to distrust and desert the one whom he ought to trust and obey. This apostasy will spread rapidly with people turning from God and against one another.

Antichrist Exalts Himself - Abomination of Desolation

Verse 4 of 2 Thessalonians chapter 2 tells us what the antichrist will do. He will oppose and exalt himself above all that is called God (or that is worshiped) and will sit as God in the temple of God, showing himself that he is God. Paul had told them this while he was still with them (v 5). This specific event is called 'the abomination of desolation' and will occur at the halfway point of the seventieth-week of Daniel (Dan. 9:27; Matt. 24:15). This will begin the great tribulation or great persecution of believers (Matt. 24:21; Rev. 13:7).

The pre-tribulation argument says that the entire seventieth-week of Daniel is God's wrath and that the church will not be on earth during this time of tribulation. They will incorrectly say that God's wrath and Satan's wrath go on at the same time or even are the same. But what does Scripture say? Concerning the day of the Lord, Isaiah 2:17 NKJV says, 'The loftiness of man shall be bowed down, and the haughtiness of men shall be brought low; *The LORD alone will be exalted in that day*' (emphasis added). Yet we just saw that the antichrist '*opposes and exalts himself above all that is called God or that is worshiped, so that he sits as God in the temple of God, showing himself that he is God.*' Daniel 11:36 NKJV says, 'Then the king (antichrist) shall do according to his own will: *he shall exalt and magnify himself above every god*, shall speak blasphemies against the God of gods, and shall prosper till the wrath has been accomplished; for what has been determined shall be done' (emphasis added). The antichrist will exalt himself during the tribulation, but at the coming (*parousia*) of Christ, God alone will be exalted. Scripture proves that these two events cannot possibly be the same.

Verses 6 and 7 mention a restraining or holding back of this lawless man of sin (antichrist). Even though the mystery of the lawless one is at work, the antichrist will not be revealed until He who restrains is taken out of the way. I am glad the Thessalonians knew who was restraining, but today, we are not sure. Yes, there are many different ideas on who is doing the restraining. The main ones are human government, the church, or the Holy Spirit. Yet none of these is ever called the restrainer in Scripture. The most popular candidate for the restrainer is the Holy Spirit (since the Holy Spirit indwells believers, the church is included with this). Yes, the Holy Spirit does convict the world of sin, and righteousness, and of judgment (John 16:8), but it is never called the restrainer. However, there is one who is called the restrainer in Scripture. I learned it from Marvin Rosenthal's teaching; I believe it to be the best explanation for who the restrainer is.

Who or What is Restraining?

Let us take a look at Marvin Rosenthal's explanation.[2] In Daniel 10:20-21 NKJV it says, 'Then he said, 'Do you know why I have come to you?' And now I must return to fight with the prince of Persia; and when I have gone forth, indeed the prince of Greece will come. But I will tell you what is noted in the Scripture of Truth. *No one upholds me against these, except Michael your prince.*' The Hebrew word used here for *upholds* is *chazaq* (Strong's #2388), which means *bind, conquer, or restrains*. Clearly we see the archangel Michael identified in Scripture as the *only one who actively restrains*. Keep in mind that the antichrist exalts himself at the halfway point of the seventieth-week of Daniel, causing the abomination of desolation. So, we should expect the restrainer to be taken out of the way at that time. Daniel 12:1a NKJV says, 'At that time Michael shall *stand up*, The great prince *who stands watch over the sons of your people (Israel)*; And there shall be a time of trouble, Such as never was since there was a nation, Even to that time.' '*At that time*' refers to the tribulation period before the day of the Lord. So during that time, Michael will *stand up*, the Hebrew word for *stand up* is *amad* (Strong's #5975), which means to *stand*. Yet, it says that Michael is the one who already actively stands watch over Israel. Now, if he is already *standing* and he *stands up*, it means that he will *stand still* and cease his upholding (restraining). Now what is really amazing is what happens after Michael stops restraining. We find that there will be a time of trouble such as never was since there was a nation, even to that time. This could only be referring to the great tribulation (Matt. 24:21; Mark 13:19) when the lawless one (the antichrist) will be revealed (2 Thess. 2:8).

At the appearance of Christ, the antichrist will be *destroyed* with the brightness of His coming (v 8b). The Greek word used here for *destroyed* is *katargeo* (Strong's #2673), which literally means *to reduce to inactivity or to render useless*. So the antichrist's power over the world will be brought to nothing at Christ's coming (*parousia*), which is associated with the day of the Lord and the rapture. The object of the antichrist's persecution, the saints, will have been removed.

Great Signs and Lying Wonders

'The *coming of the lawless one (the antichrist)* is according to the *working of Satan, with all power, signs, and lying wonders, and with all unrighteous deception among those who perish,* because they did not receive the love of the truth, that they might be saved' (2 Thess. 2:9-10 NKJV, emphasis added). The antichrist will be empowered by Satan. He and his false prophet will deceive many with great signs and wonders, if it were possible, even the elect (saints) would be deceived (Matt. 24:24; Mark 13:22; Rev. 13:13-15). Only the unsaved will believe the signs and worship the antichrist (2 Thess. 2:10; Rev. 13:8).

A Strong Delusion

The last two verses that we will cover are hard to swallow, but it is important that we get an understanding. When the restrainer is removed at the midpoint of the seventieth-week of Daniel, the antichrist will be revealed and will exalt himself above all that is called God. This will begin the great tribulation, the persecution of the nation of Israel and the church (Matt. 24:21). The falling away from the faith will occur (2 Thess. 2:3). The antichrist and his false prophet will perform great signs and wonders (2 Thess. 2:9). All those who do not receive the love of the truth to be saved will believe these signs and wonders (2 Thess. 2:10). '*For this reason God will send them strong delusion*, that they should believe *the lie*, that they all may be condemned who did not believe the truth but had pleasure in unrighteousness' (verses 11-12). Yes, God will send this strong delusion. I do not believe that anyone will be on the fence. Nor will there be a great revival. You will either worship the antichrist and receive his mark to spare your life only to later receive the wrath of God and eternal condemnation (Rev. 14:9-11) or you will *refuse* to worship the antichrist, *refuse* his mark and stay faithful to Christ and pay for it with your life or your freedom (Rev. 6:9; 12:17; 13:7; 14:12-13). This will be a time of testing.

Those who have refused to love the truth will believe '*the lie.*' This is a specific lie that they will believe. I am not sure what 'the lie' is; however, it is possible that '*the lie*' is that the man of sin, the son of perdition, the antichrist who will exalt and show himself to be God is God. Only those whose name is written in the book of life will not believe this lie.

An Overall Review

The following is a general overview of what we learned in the chapter. Second Thessalonians the first chapter gave an overview of what would happen when Christ is revealed. It is as follows:

- Persecution and tribulation of the saints, (v 4)
  When the Lord is revealed (v 7) [also called the day of the Lord] *He will*
1. Repay with tribulation those who trouble the saints (v 6)
2. Take vengeance on those who do not know God (v 8)

3. Give rest to those who are troubled [the persecuted saints] (v 7)

Before the coming (*parousia*) of Christ, the day of the Lord, and the gathering together can come, these events must happen (2 Thess. 2:1-11)

- He who restrains is taken out of the way (v 7)
- Apostasy (v 3)
- Man of sin, son of perdition (the antichrist) is revealed (v 3)
- The antichrist exalts himself, sits as God, and demands worship (v 4)
- Great signs and lying wonders are performed (v 9)
- Strong delusion from God; all who take pleasure in unrighteous will be condemned (v 11)

At the Lord's coming (v 15),

- The dead in Christ rise first (1 Thess. 4:15)
- Those who are alive and remain (survive) are caught up together to meet the Lord in the air (v 17)

Chapter 8

Revelation 3:10

[10] 'Because thou hast *kept* the word of my patience, I also will *keep* thee *from* the hour of *temptation,* which shall come upon all the world, to try them that dwell upon the earth.' (Rev. 3:10 KJV, emphasis added)

[10] 'Because you have *kept* My command to *persevere,* I also will *keep* you *from* the hour of *trial* which shall come upon the whole world, to test those who dwell on the earth.' (Rev. 3:10 NKJV, emphasis added)

There are three main Scriptures that are used in support of the pre-tribulation rapture argument (1 Thess. 5:9; Rom 5:9; and Rev. 3:10). 1 Thessalonians 5:9 and Romans 5:9 both say that we (believers) are not appointed unto God's wrath. Those in Christ are not appointed to God's wrath because Jesus has already received the wrath of God at Calvary on behalf of all believers. Only unbelievers will receive God's wrath. Therefore, our main focus will be Revelation 3:10.

Chapters 2 and 3 of the book of Revelation cover seven letters addressed to seven actual churches located in Asia Minor (today it is called Turkey) between 60AD and 95AD, most believe 95AD. Some hold that the churches are examples of churches throughout church history and some feel that they even address specific issues with people in the church today. I believe this to have some merit. In general, each letter commends, criticizes, and instructs each church. Promises are given to the overcomers. The overcomers are those who heed instructions and persevere. Only one church (Laodicea), the last mentioned, received no commendations and two churches (Smyrna and Philadelphia) received no criticism. Revelation 3:10 is a verse from the letter to the church in Philadelphia. This church is described as being faithful, having kept Christ's word and not denying Christ's name.

The pre-tribulationist views Revelation 3:10 as the nail in the coffin for their argument. This is because it says that I will keep you from the hour of trial. It is interpreted in the pre-tribulational rapture view that the church will be removed from the earth before the 70th week of Daniel begins (also called by many the 7-year tribulation period). This view takes that to mean that the church will be removed (raptured) from the earth before the tribulation or the rule of the antichrist begins, even before the first seal is broken in Revelation 6. It is also thought that the rapture will be signless and could happen at any moment. However, in using this reasoning, all other warnings given to the churches are ignored.

To the church in Sardis, Jesus says, be watchful (3:2a) and in verse 3b He says if you will not watch, I will come upon you as a thief, and you will not know what hour I will come upon you. Jesus also gives the same instruction in the Olivet Discourse in Matthew 24:42; 25:13; Mark 13:35, 37; Luke 21:36; later in Revelation 16:15; and other places in Scripture. If the rapture is signless, then what are we commanded to watch for? As we have seen throughout this book, there are signs associated with the return of Christ, the end of the age, and the day of the Lord. We are to watch for signs. To the church in Smyrna, He says in chapter 2 verse 10 NKJV, 'Do not fear any of those things which you are about to *suffer*. Indeed the devil is about to throw some of you into *prison*, that you may be *tested*, and you will have *tribulation ten days*. Be faithful until death, and I will give you the crown of life' (emphasis added). Does that sound like the church will not endure any tribulation or any part of the tribulation to come? Scripture says that the antichrist, who will be controlled by Satan, will persecute the saints. Next let us take a look at our Scripture passage in context before examining Revelation 3:10 specifically. Afterwards, we will examine Revelation 3:10 in three different translations (emphasis added in each).

⁷ 'And to the angel of the church in Philadelphia write; These things saith he that is holy, he that is true, he that hath the key of David, he that openeth, and no man shutteth; and shutteth, and no man openeth; ⁸I know thy works: behold, I have set before thee an open door, and no man can shut it: for thou hast a little strength, and hast kept my word, and hast not denied my name. ⁹Behold, I will make them of the synagogue of Satan, which say they are Jews, and are not, but do lie; behold, I will make them to come and worship before thy feet, and to know that I have loved thee. ¹⁰*Because thou hast kept the word of my patience, I also will keep thee from the hour of temptation, which shall come upon all the world, to try them that dwell upon the earth.* ¹¹Behold, I come quickly: hold that fast which thou hast, that no man take thy crown. ¹²Him that overcometh will I make a pillar in the temple of my God, and he shall go no more out: and I will write upon him the name of my God, and the name of the city of my God, which is new Jerusalem, which cometh down out of heaven from my God: and I will write upon him my new name. ¹³He that hath an ear, let him hear what the Spirit saith unto the churches.' (Rev. 3:7-13 KJV, emphasis added)

¹⁰ 'Because thou hast *kept* the word of my *patience*, I also will *keep* thee *from* the hour of *temptation*, which shall come upon all the world, to try them that dwell upon the earth.' (Rev. 3:10 KJV, emphasis added)

¹⁰ 'Because you have *kept* My command to *persevere*, I

also will *keep* you *from* the hour of *trial* which shall come upon the whole world, to test those who dwell on the earth.' (Rev. 3:10 NKJV, emphasis added)

[10] 'Since you have *kept* my command to *endure patiently*, I will also *keep* you *from* the hour of *trial* that is going to come upon the whole world to test those who live on the earth.' (Rev. 3:10 NIV, emphasis added)

Understanding Key Greek Words in Revelation 3:10 and their Meanings

Since the book of Revelation was originally written in Greek, it is important that we gain a clear understanding of the key Greek words used in this verse. We will also compare the way these same words are used elsewhere in Scripture. The context and meaning of these words will help us understand the message that the Holy Spirit intended its readers to get. It is important to note that Greek is a very precise language. Almost every word has a very precise or specific meaning.

'Because you have ***kept***....I will also ***keep***......'
Kept / Keep: *tereo*, (Strong's #5083) means to *guard* or *protect from loss, to watch over or preserve*. It also means *to observe, to give heed to* (as of keeping commandments). The meaning depends on the context in which it is used.

'kept My command to ***persevere***....'
Persevere: *hupomone*, (Strong's #5281) means *endurance, continue to wait patiently*. It literally comes from two Greek words, *hupo*, meaning *under or beneath* and *meno*, meaning *to continue to abide, dwell or remain* (endure). Putting these words together, we have *hupomeno*, meaning *to remain under, to endure patiently, to have fortitude, to persevere while undergoing trials*.

'keep you ***from*** the hour....'

From: *ek*, (Strong's #1537) which means *out of*. *Ek* carries a starting point from within (originating from inside of a place and traveling out of it or being guarded from something while remaining inside of it). This is different from another Greek word that is commonly translated *from*. The word is *apo*, which means *from*. *Apo* has the idea of originating outside something and moving away from it - never having been inside. In the English translation, this difference is not seen.

'from the hour of ***trial***......'

Trial: *peirasmos*, (Strong's #3986) *a putting to proof by testing or tempting, temptation.*

'Because you have *kept* My command to *persevere*'

Kept (tereo) and Persevere (hupomone)

The word *Because*, used in this verse, points to a condition that has been met to receive a certain response. The Greek word is *hoti* (Strong's #3748) used here causatively, *because*, a 'cause and effect.' One thing has to happen for another thing to occur. Meaning, since you have done that, I will do this (of course, this could have positive or negative consequences). It is obvious that one party must meet a condition before the promise can be granted (reward or punishment) to the other. *So, in context of the end times, what is the condition that needs to be met to receive this promise?* According to our study verse, they have ***kept*** the word of my patience (KJV), My command to persevere in the NKJV, and my command to endure patiently (NIV).

The Greek word for '**kept**' and 'keep' in verse 10, as previously mentioned is *tereo*, meaning, *to guard, to watch over*. It also means, *to observe as in keeping commandments* (depending on the context that it is being used). There is a difference in hearing a command and heeding to or obeying a command. James 1:22 KJV commands believers to 'Be ye doers of the word, and not hearers only, deceiving your own selves.' We deceive ourselves when we only hear the word and do not obey or heed it.

In its first appearance, *tereo* in verse 10, says 'because you have *kept* my (Christ's) command to persevere,' meaning *to observe,* as of keeping commandments. We find it used in the same context in Revelation 1:3; 2:26; and 3:8.

[3] 'Blessed *is* he who reads and those who hear the words of this prophecy, and *keep (observe)* those things which are written in it; for the time *is* near.' (Rev. 1:3 NKJV, emphasis added)

[26] 'And he who overcomes, and *keeps (observes)* My works until the end, to him I will give power over the nations.' (Rev. 2:26 NKJV, emphasis added)

[8] 'I know your works. See, I have set before you an open door, and no one can shut it; for you have a little strength, have *kept (observed)* My word, and have not denied My name.' (Rev. 3:8 NKJV, emphasis added)

Persevere, *hupomeno,* which literally means *to continue to endure patiently while undergoing trial or suffering.* From Revelation 3 verse 8, we can also see that the same individuals that Jesus is addressing did not deny Christ's name. It is easy to see that there is obvious pressure on them to deny the name of Christ and the faith involved. In the context of verse 10 (future/end times), there will be great pressure to deny the name of Christ. So literally, He is saying, '*Because you have observed my command to continue to endure patiently while undergoing great trials.*' Keep in mind that during the 70th week of Daniel, the antichrist will apply extreme pressure to believers to deny Christ's name. He (the antichrist) will demand allegiance, forcing many to take his mark or face the consequences (Rev.13:7,15). All who receive his mark will receive the wrath of God (Rev. 14:9-11). However, the saints are told to keep the commandments of God and the faith of Jesus (Rev. 14:12-13). Paul prayed that the Thessalonians would have the patience of Christ (2 Thess. 3:5) when they faced persecution. During the time of Satan's wrath, many or most of the saints will be killed or imprisoned by the antichrist for taking a stand and not receiving his mark, but these overcomers will be rewarded. The faithful or persevering group of believers addressed in Rev. 3:10 will be the ones kept from the hour of trial.

I also will *keep* you *from* the hour of *trial*

Keep (tereo)

In its second appearance in the same verse 'I will also *keep* you from the hour,' the Greek word is *tereo*, which in context means *to watch over or guard* (to protect), as in being divinely preserved. To be divinely preserved or protected, one does not have to be removed from the earth. Many believe that it means to be removed from the earth. However, that is not the case here. We find the same word used this way when Jesus prayed for the disciples in John 17:11-12, and 15.

In verse 15 of the 17th chapter of John NKJV, Jesus prayed,

'I do not pray that You should take them (the disciples) *out of* (*ek*) the world, but that You should *keep* (*tereo*) them *from* (*ek*) the evil one.'

The NIV translates the same verse this way,

'My prayer is not that you take them out of the world but that you **protect** them from the evil one.'

Jesus did not pray that they be removed from the world, but that they be *protected* from the evil one while remaining on the earth. There is an obvious difference between totally removing one out of the world and *protecting someone from danger while remaining in the world*, as we see clearly in John 17:15. The evil one is none other than Satan, the devil, who of course will empower the antichrist during the 70th week of Daniel.

Years ago, I read utility meters as part of my job. I would have to go in and out of yards from house to house. Some yards had dogs in them. Now, I love dogs, but some dogs were vicious and would bite if given a chance. I would encounter many dogs that would be chained or behind a fence. I always preferred them behind a fence. A chain-link fence gave me a great sense of security. I felt protected as long as I remained where the protection was. I could stand behind a fence with the most vicious dog barking in my face, yet, I felt no fear. It is amazing how much confidence a fence gave me, but without it, I would have been in trouble. Just as that fence provided protection for me, God can and will provide protection for this specific faithful group of believers on earth who have kept His command to endure patiently.

From (ek) the hour

Let us take another look at John 17, but this time we will examine the use of the word *from,* the Greek word *ek*, meaning *out of*, the same Greek word used in Revelation 3:10.

In verse 15, Jesus prayed,

'I do not pray that You should take them (the disciples) *out of* (*ek*) the world, but that You should *keep* (*tereo*) them *from (ek)* the evil one.'

The NIV translates the same verse this way,

'My prayer is not that you take them *out of* the world but that you *protect* them *from* the evil one.'

We see here that Jesus did not pray that the disciples be removed from the earth, but that they may be protected *from* the evil one (Satan) while still remaining on earth. Compare the second part of our key verse again. 'I also will *keep* you *from* the hour of trial' (Rev. 3:10b). We have already looked at the two Greek words for *from* in the section about *ek* and *apo*. These words are called prepositions (they are used with nouns and help form phases). We saw that although they are both translated *from, apo* has the idea of originating outside something and moving away from it (never having been inside). We see this difference elsewhere in Scripture. For instance, 1 Thessalonians 1:10 says: 'And to wait for His Son *from (ek)* heaven, whom He raised *from (ek)* the dead, *even* Jesus who delivers us *from (apo)* the wrath to come.'

Notice, speaking of Christ, *from (ek)* heaven and *from (ek)* the dead, He was indeed in heaven, but came to earth. Christ also came from the dead to be resurrected. In both instances, the Greek word *ek* is used. However, in the same verse when speaking of God's wrath, it says: Jesus who delivers us *from (apo)* the wrath to come. The Greek word *apo* is used, which means that those who trust in Christ will be removed before God's wrath begins (never being inside of or experiencing God's wrath). The Greek perfectly reveals this. This also lines up with 1 Thessalonians 5:9 and Romans 5:9 which of course says the believers are not appointed to God's wrath. Keep in mind that the tribulation and God's wrath are two separate events. Now, if Revelation 3:10 were really saying that the church would be removed from earth before the hour of trial or temptation begins, would not the Holy Spirit have guided the apostle John to use the word *apo* instead of *ek*? According to *Vincent's Word Studies* on Revelation 3:10: '*From the hour*' The preposition implies, not a keeping *from* temptation, but a keeping *in* temptation, as the result of which they shall be delivered *out of* its power. Compare John 17:15.' [1] (We have already compared the use of 'from' in John 17:15). Referring to the great multitude that appear in heaven just before God's wrath begins (Rev. 7:9-17), verse 14 says these are the ones who come *out of (ek)* the great tribulation. They were in the great tribulation, but came out of it.

Imagine you and a friend take a trip to the grocery store. Your friend drives there but stays in the car. You go inside, purchase a few items and come out of the store. You return home and a neighbor asks where both of you have been. You both say that you are just returning from the grocery store. Now, since you actually went inside; you are returning *from (ek)* the grocery store and your friend who did not actually enter the store is returning *from (apo)* the grocery store.

From the hour of *trial*

Trial (peirasmos)
Now we have come to the final key Greek word in our study verse. It is *trial (peiasmos)*, 'I also will keep you from the hour of

trial which shall come upon the whole world.' The Greek word for *trial* is *peirasmos*, which means a *putting to proof or test* (by good or evil), *experience, temptation* (by implication adversity). In the KJV, *trial* is translated as *temptation*. Of course, it is not hard to see the similarity of the two words. In fact, *peirasmos* (trial/temptation) comes from *peirazo* (tempt). James uses this same basic Greek word when he speaks of trials. According to James, God does not tempt men with evil.

> [12] 'Blessed *is* the man who *endures temptation*; for when he has been approved, he will receive the crown of life which the Lord has promised to those who love Him. [13]Let no one say when he is *tempted*, 'I am *tempted* by God'; for God cannot be tempted by evil, nor does He Himself *tempt* anyone.' (James 1:12-13 NKJV, emphasis added)

The word *tempt* or *tempter* is the Greek word *peirazo* (Strong's #3985), which means to *test, scrutinize, entice, examine,* or *prove.* 1 Thessalonians 3:5 translates it as *tempter* (the devil) and Matthew 4:1 translates it as *tempted.* This hour of *trial* is a time of testing for the believer and even in some ways the unbelievers on earth. Even though Satan is given authority to make war against the saints (Rev. 13:7), it is not the wrath of God. This time of testing during the end times will reveal who the true believers are and not. The true believers will choose to endure persecution for the name of Christ rather than submit to the antichrist, but the unbelieving world and the mere members of the church without true faith in Christ (a.k.a. church folks or pew warmers) will follow the antichrist.

For My Name's Sake

Make no mistake, those who name the name of Christ will have to endure much for the sake of Jesus' name. Jesus did say that the elect would be delivered up to *tribulation, killed,* and *hated* by all nations for His name's sake (Matt. 24:9); *hated* (Matt. 10:22; Mark 13:13); *persecuted* and *imprisoned* (Luke 21:12). The apostle John, who penned the book of Revelation, was imprisoned on the island of Patmos for the word of God and the testimony of Jesus Christ (Rev. 1:9). As mentioned earlier, the church of Smyrna would suffer imprisonment, be tested, and have tribulation (Rev. 2:10).

Jesus said, he who *endures* to the end will be saved (*delivered*) (Matt. 10:22; 24:13; Mark 13:13). *Endures* is the same basic Greek word as *persevere* in Revelation 3:10 (*hupomemo- endures patiently while undergoing a trial*). As we saw earlier, the word *saved* in this instance means *delivered* (*sozo - delivered*). Saved (delivered) here means to be delivered from persecution (rescued). In Revelation 2:10c-11, the church (of Smyrna) is also told to be faithful until death and they will not be harmed by the second death.

Why is it that the church today separates itself from the apostles and the early believers who endured great persecution for Jesus' name's sake? Why does the church also separate itself from the persecuted elect mentioned in Matthew 24; Mark 13; and Luke 21; the persecuted saints mention in Revelation; and all but one of the seven churches in the book of Revelation? Are we not called soldiers (2 Tim. 2:3-4)?

> [3] 'Thou therefore endure hardness, as a good soldier of Jesus Christ. [4]No man that warreth entangleth himself with the affairs of this life; that he may please him who hath chosen him to be a soldier.' (2 Tim. 2:3-4 KJV)

A combat soldier *expects* hardship and is prepared to endure it; he expects to be fired upon in battle and encounter the enemy face to face. It is what he trains for. His desire is to please his commanding officer.

Believers Exempt from God's Wrath

Scripture is clear. The believer is not to experience God's wrath.

[9] 'Much more then, being now justified by his blood, we shall be saved *from (apo) wrath* through him.' (Rom. 5:9 KJV, emphasis added)

[9] 'For God hath not appointed us to wrath, but to obtain salvation by our Lord Jesus Christ.' (1 Thess. 5:9 KJV)

According to Romans 5:9, believers will be saved *from (apo)* God's wrath. *Apo* is used, meaning *from* and not having entered in God's wrath. The divine retribution is appointed to the ungodly. As seen in the previous chapter, the principle of divine retribution is called *lex talionsis* ('an eye for an eye, a tooth for a tooth'), and is seen many times in Scripture (Is. 66:6; 2 Thess. 1:6-10; 2 Pet. 2:9; and Rev: 13:10). According to 2 Peter 2:9, the Lord knows how to *deliver* the godly *out of (ek) temptations (peirasmos)* and to reserve the unjust under punishment for the Day of Judgment. As we see here again, the godly will experience temptation (trial, tribulation) but will be delivered out of it. God's wrath/judgment is reserved for the ungodly.

What have We Learned?

I know that this chapter may have been somewhat technical; however, I believe it was necessary for us to get an accurate understanding of what Revelation 3:10 is truly saying. This verse is considered to be the primary verse for the pre-tribulation argument. However, our closer examination proved it to be otherwise. We found that the promise from Christ in Revelation 3:10 was given because a condition was met. It was *not* saying that the church would be removed from earth before the tribulation began. In examining the Greek, we saw that what He actually promised was protection during this time. In other words, 'Because you have kept my commandment to endure persecution patiently, I will protect you during the time of testing that will come to test the whole world.'

Chapter 9

Answering the Strongest Points of the Pre-tribulation View

In this chapter, I will address what the pre-tribulation proponents believe are their strongest supporting points. I agree that on the surface, they seem to be very strong points. Yet, after careful study, I found that there were weakness and inconsistencies.

Pre-tribulation Point One:

John represents the church being raptured in Revelation chapter four.

The Scripture that I am speaking of is Revelation 4:1-4 KJV. It reads as follows:

> [1] 'After this I looked, and, behold, a door was opened in heaven: and the first voice which *I heard was as it were of a trumpet talking with me*; which said, *Come up hither,* and *I will show thee things which must be*

hereafter. [2]And *immediately I was in the spirit:* and, behold, a throne was *set in heaven,* and one sat on the throne. [3]And he that sat was to look upon like a jasper and a sardine stone: and there was a rainbow round about the throne, in sight like unto an emerald. [4]And round about the throne were four and twenty seats: and upon the seats *I saw four and twenty elders sitting, clothed in white raiment; and they had on their heads crowns of gold.'* (emphasis added)

Several assumptions are drawn from this passage of Scripture. Because John is called up to heaven after the letters to the seven churches, it is assumed that John represents the church being raptured after the church age. It is also said that the 24 elders represent the church, because of their white raiment and crowns. I was taught this as a former pre-tribulationist. It seemed true to me at the time. There was the trumpet, and John was called to heaven. However, if we are true to Scripture, it does not say that John represents the church. Where in Scripture does it say that John or the 24 elders represent the church? It simply does not.

Also, because the word 'trumpet' is mentioned, it is assumed that this is the trumpet call of the rapture (1 Cor. 15:52; 1 Thess. 4:16). However, a careful read of this passage reveals that John heard a *voice,* not a trumpet. John simply compared this *voice* to a trumpet. He uses a simile. Of course, similes make direct comparisons, usually using a connecting word such as *like* or *as.* This is precisely what we find here.

If we take it upon ourselves to draw our own conclusions to what symbols or passages of Scripture mean, we can make Scripture mean whatever we want it to mean. This leads to error. Scripture must be handled very carefully. It should not be assumed that John represents the church without Scripture saying it elsewhere.

Pre-tribulation Point Two:

The word *church* or *churches* is mentioned 18 times in the first three chapters of Revelation, but not mentioned at all from chapters 4 through 21.

In chapters 1 through 3, you find the word *church* multiple times, because specific warnings and instructions are given to seven different churches. Because you do not find the word *church* mentioned between chapters 4 and 21, it is believed by the pre-tribulationalist that the church has been raptured. Although you do not find the word *church*, you do find the word *saints*. In Scripture, believers are called the elect, the church, servants, and yes, saints. Saints (*hagios* [Strong's # 40] meaning *consecrated, separated*) is mentioned 13 times from chapters 5 through 20 (Rev. 5: 8; 8:3-4; 11:18; 13:7, 10; 14:12; 15:3; 16:16; 17:6; 18:24; 19:8; and 20:9).

The word *church* indicates a large group of people, some of which are not *true* believers in Christ (i.e. 'the true church'), but just members of the group. Many may or may not be dedicated to Christ. However, the individuals who are sincere followers of Christ are 'saints.' The great persecution from the antichrist will reveal who really belongs to Christ. The *saints* will stand strong for God and not deny His name. The *saints* will keep the commandments of God, have a testimony of Jesus Christ, and become overcomers. Membership of a 'church' does not mean one will be faithful to Christ, nor does it mean that one is a 'saint.'

In the book of Revelation, you will find that the antichrist makes war against the saints. The saints are to remain patient and keep the faith (Rev. 13:10; 14:12). They (saints or servants of God) will also have the testimony of Jesus Christ (Rev. 1:2, 9; 6:9; 11:7; 12:11, 17; 19:10). Only the *true* church will keep the testimony of Jesus Christ, no one else. We also found that they are the ones who keep the commandments of God (Rev. 12:17; 14:12). John says to the church in 1 John that if we know and love God, we will keep his commandments (1 John 2:3-4; 3:22, 24; 5:2-3). Those who keep the commandments of God are blessed (Rev. 22:14).

Even though the word *church* is not found in chapters 4

through 21 of the book of Revelation, it does not mean that the church is not on earth. When the pressure and persecution begins, an apostasy will occur (2 Thess. 2:3) and only those truly faithful to God's commandments and those holding the testimony of Jesus Christ will stand firm. They will endure to the end. They are therefore called 'saints.'

It is interesting to note that the word *church* is not in any of the rapture passages in Scripture (1 Thess. 4:13-17; 1 Cor. 15:51-53; or John 14:1-3). Does that mean that the church is not included in the rapture? Of course not. Also, the church is not mentioned in chapter 20 of Revelation, which describes the millennium and never is it mentioned in chapter 21, which describes the Eternal Reign. Does that mean that the church will not be present at each of these also? Of course not. Therefore, just as chapters 20 and 21 apply to the church, so do chapters 4 through 19.

Other names for the faithful followers of Christ in the book of Revelation are as follows:

(1) 'A great multitude which no one could count' (Rev. 7:9)
(2) 'Servants' bond-servants (Rev. 11:18)
(3) 'Saints' (Rev. 13:7)
(4) The 'called, chosen, and faithful' (Rev. 17:14)
(5) 'His wife' (Rev. 19:7)

Pre-tribulation Point Three:

The church is not here during events described in the Olivet Discourse (Matthew 24).

Most pre-tribulationists adamantly argue that the church is not on earth during the events described in the Olivet Discourse. In other words, the belief is that the rapture occurs before these events. The reasoning that I was taught as a pre-tribulationist was that Matthew is the gospel to the Jews, also stating that this discourse contains references to the Sabbath and the holy place (temple) in Jerusalem, which does not concern the church. Yes, for believers in Jesus Christ, Jesus is our Sabbath (Col. 2:16-17), and we are the temples of the Holy Spirit (1 Cor. 6:19). However, the references to the Sabbath and the temple in Matthew 24 merely point to Jerusalem as being the starting point of the great tribulation or worldwide persecution of all who refuse to submit to the rule of the antichrist.

The gospel of Mark is addressed mainly to the Romans or Gentiles. Nevertheless, even though it does not mainly address a Jewish audience, Mark 13 still records the Olivet Discourse. So we have a Gentile gospel that contains the Olivet Discourse. Therefore, we cannot legitimately remove the church from the Olivet Discourse. A noticeable difference is that Mark does not make a reference to the Sabbath or the holy place (temple). Yet in verse 11 of Mark 13, Jesus does refer to the Holy Spirit at work on earth during that time.

Although Matthew is considered the Jewish gospel, as we have seen earlier, it is interesting to note that Matthew is the only gospel that specifically mentions the church. There are three clear references to the church (Matt. 16:18; 18:17 [twice]). Also, in the Great Commission (Matt. 28:18-20), it is widely held that Jesus was referring to the church. Why is Matthew the only gospel that it is found in? Now, if with the book of Matthew, Jesus prophesied about an entity called the church (Matt. 16:18), instructed the church (Matt. 18:17), and commissioned the church (Matt. 28:18-20, the Great Commission), how can those who hold the pre-tribulation view legitimately exclude the church from the Olivet Discourse on the basis of it being a Jewish gospel?

It is also widely held in the pre-tribulation community that John 14:1-3, refers to the rapture. Jesus spoke those words no more than two days after He gave the Olivet Discourse to the same Jewish disciples. If Jesus was speaking to the same Jewish disciples about His return during the same week, why is he referring to the church during one conversion and not the church during the other? Initially the church, which these same disciples would begin, was 100% Jewish.

As I have already said, the pre-tribulation view holds that the church is raptured before the tribulation begins. Yet, in Matthew 28:20, Jesus said that He would be with the church until the end of the age. But what is the end of age you might ask? In Matthew 13:39, Jesus states that the harvest occurs at the end of the age. The harvest is of course the rapture. So it can be established that Jesus will be with the believers on earth until the rapture, which occurs at the end of the age. Now, in Matthew 24:3, the disciples ask for the sign of Jesus' coming (*parousia*) and the end of the age, which means that the end of the age (the rapture) is associated with a sign. In verse 6, (after several events described in the Olivet Discourse) Jesus plainly says that the end of the age will not occur at that point. Not until verse 14 do you see the end of the age. If that is the case, then how can the rapture be signless or occur at any moment? Verses 4 through 14 reveal the overview of the 70th week of Daniel. Verse 15 picks up back at the middle of the 70th week of Daniel. See the chapter on Matthew 24 for more detail.

Pre-tribulation Point Four:

The Second Coming (*Parousia*) of Christ is not the rapture.

The pre-tribualtionist frequently says that Christ comes for the church at the rapture and with the church at His second coming. If you read the section in chapter five on the coming (*parousia*) of Christ, you already know that the coming (*parousia*) of Christ is Christ's future presence on earth (which begins at the rapture). There is only one second coming of Christ, not a second and a third. When Scripture refers to Christ's second coming, the emphasis is sometimes on the rapture and other times on the day of the Lord.

1 Thessalonians 4:15 KJV says, 'For this we say unto you by the word of the Lord, that we which are alive and remain unto the *coming* (*parousia*) of the Lord shall not prevent them which are asleep.' The true church or saints will be here until Christ's coming (*parousia*), which is associated with a sign (Matt. 24:3).

2 Thessalonians 2:1-2 KJV says, 'Now we beseech you,

brethren, by the *coming* (*parousia*) of our Lord Jesus Christ, and *by* our *gathering together* (*episunagôge* [Strong #1997] which means a complete *collection* or *assembling* [gathering] together) unto him, That ye be not soon shaken in mind, or be troubled, neither by spirit, nor by word, nor by letter as from us, as that the day of Christ is at hand.' This is a clear association of Christ's second coming with the rapture. The rapture occurs *at* the second coming of Christ.

There will be a gathering together of believers at the rapture. From the Greek word *episunago*, translated *gather together* in Matthew 24:31 and Mark 13:27. Speaking of the same time, Luke 21:28 says, 'And when these things begin to come to pass, then look up, and lift up your heads; for your redemption draweth nigh (near).' In addition, Ephesians 4:30 says that we are sealed until the day of redemption.

Pre-tribulation Point Five:

The Holy Spirit is the restrainer and is removed with the church at the rapture.

It is said that because individuals in the church house the Holy Spirit, it restrains evil. It is also said that if the church is removed, the Holy Spirit is removed along with its restraining power; therefore, the Holy Spirit is the restrainer described in 2 Thessalonians 2:7. Yes, the Holy Spirit does convict the world of sin, righteousness, and judgment (John 16:8). However, how can the Holy Spirit be removed? It is God who sustains all life, space, and time. 'For in Him we live and move and have our being' (Acts 17: 28a NKJV). Think about it. If it were possible for the Holy Spirit to really be removed, all would die.

Wickedness has been on earth since the fall of man. We have seen horrible wickedness expressed over the years. The list includes Haman's attempt to destroy the Jews (in the book of Esther) to the horrors under Antiochus Epiphanes (approx. 165BC) to Hitler's attempt to destroy the Jews during the Holocaust, to the worldwide brutal ethnic cleansing, and even to the silent screams of the aborted unborn in the United States. Let us face it; the wickedness in the world continues to increase even though the Holy Spirit convicts the world of sin, righteousness, and judgment. Jeremiah 17:9 NKJV talks about mankind's heart by saying, 'The heart is deceitful above all things, and desperately wicked; who can know it?'

Like Matthew 24, the 13th chapter of Mark also contains the Olivet Discourse. Of course, according to the pre-tribulationist, during that time, the church has already been raptured and the Holy Spirit has been removed from earth. Now, if that were the case, why does Mark 13:11 NKJV say, 'But when they arrest you and deliver you up, do not worry beforehand, or premeditate what you will speak. But whatever is given you in that hour, speak that; for it is not you who speak, but the *Holy Spirit*'? If the Holy Spirit is the restrainer and is gone, how can He be speaking for believers on earth during this time of tribulation that Jesus described in this previous verse? If you choose to believe that the restrainer is the Holy Spirit and that He is removed when the church is raptured, that is fine, but now you have just placed the church on earth during the Olivet Discourse the 70th week of Daniel (which includes the time of tribulation).

*See the chapter on 2 Thessalonians for more information on the restrainer.

Pre-tribulation Point Six:

Matthew 24:36-44 describes the wicked being taken to judgment before the millennium begins.

> 36 'But of that day and hour knoweth no man, no, not the angels of heaven, but my Father only. 37But as the days of Noe (Noah) were, so shall also the coming of the Son of man be. 38For as in the days that were before the flood they were eating and drinking, marrying and giving in marriage, until the day that Noe (Noah) entered into the ark, 39And

knew not until the flood came, and *took* them all away; so shall also the coming of the Son of man be. [40]Then shall two be in the field; the one shall be *taken*, and the other *left*. [41]Two women shall be grinding at the mill; the one shall be *taken*, and the other *left*. [42]Watch therefore: for ye know not what hour your Lord doth come. [43]But know this, that if the goodman of the house had known in what watch the thief would come, he would have watched, and would not have suffered his house to be broken up. [44]Therefore be ye also ready: for in such an hour as ye think not the Son of man cometh.' (Matt. 24:36-44 KJV, emphasis added)

The Greek language used does not allow for the interpretation that many pre-tribulationist hold. The Greek word for *took* in verse 39 is different from the Greek words for *taken* in verses 40 and 41 in the same chapter. When referring to the days of Noah (verses 36-39), speaking of the flood that 'came and *took* them all away,' the Greek word is *airo* (Strong's #142), which means *take up or away*. It refers to those who perished in the flood. Yet when referring to the coming of the Son of Man (Jesus) (verses 39b-44), the word for *taken* is *paralambano*, which means to *receive alongside* or *to receive to ones self*. This obviously carries a totally different meaning than the pre-tribulationist would lead you to believe. The same Greek word *paralambano* is used by Jesus in John 14:1-3, '...I will come again and *receive* you to Myself; that where I am, there you may be also.' *Paralambano* is clearly an endearing term used to describe those received alongside Jesus at the rapture. Most pre-tribulationist view John 14:1-3 as a rapture passage. The word for *left* in the Greek describes the very opposite of what the word for *taken* does. The Greek word for *left* in verses 40 through 41 is *aphiemi* (Strong's #863), which means to *forsake, layside, neglect, or disregard*. A better translation for verses 40 and 41 would read, 'Then two men will be in the field: one will be *received* and the other *forsaken*. Two women will be grinding at the mill: one will be *received* and the other *forsaken*.'

Matthew 24:39b-44 simply does not and cannot be describing the wicked being taken to judgment at the beginning of the millennium. These verses could only be describing the rapture of the church. See the chapter on Matthew 24 for more information on this.

Pre-tribulation Point Seven:

God's wrath begins with the first seal in Revelation 6.

Both those who hold the pre-tribulation view and the pre-wrath view agree that the church is not appointed to God's wrath (1 Thess. 1:9-10 and 1 Thess. 5:9). The difference here concerns timing of when God's wrath actually begins.

In the pre-tribulation book *The Truth Behind Left Behind* by Mark Hitchcock and Thomas Ice, introduction by Tim LaHaye, they write in chapter 2, page 33, 'The nature of the entire Tribulation period is one of pounding judgment against a rebellious world. The Judgment of God begins with the first seal that is opened in Revelation 6:1 and continues all the way until the Second Coming in Revelation 19:11-21. To say the God's wrath is confined to the very end of the Tribulation (as the Pre-Wrath view maintains), one must overlook the fact that all of the seal judgments are opened by the Lamb (Revelation 6:1). They are the wrath of God against sinful man, and they are opened at the very beginning of the Tribulation. The very nature and purpose of the entire Tribulation period demands that Christ's bride be caught away and delivered from this time of trouble.

Genesis 18-19, which records the rescue of Lot and his family from Sodom, clearly teaches that it is against God's character to destroy the righteous with the wicked when He pours out His judgment. The rapture of Enoch to heaven before the flood is another illustration of this principle (Genesis 5:24).' [1]

If you have read and understand the previous chapters in this book, you can easily point out the inaccurate sections of this quote. I will briefly point out some of them.

Revelation 6: 9-11 NKJV describes what happens at the opening of the 5th seal, the souls under the altar that had been killed by the antichrist (beast) are asking God to avenge their blood. It reads, 'When He opened the fifth seal, I saw under the altar the souls of those who had been slain for the word of God and for the testimony which they held. And they cried with a loud voice, saying, 'How long, O Lord, holy and true, until You judge and avenge our blood on those who dwell on the earth?' Then a white robe was given to each of them; and it was said to them that they should rest a little while longer, until both *the number of* their fellow servants and their brethren, who would be killed as they *were,* was completed.'

If the seals are God's wrath, then why are the souls under the altar crying for their blood to be avenged (Rev. 6:9-11). In fact, the souls are asking God when will His wrath begin on earth. More would be killed as they were before God's wrath would begin on earth. Is God killing the righteous? No. Then how can the seals be God's judgment on the wicked if only the godly are being persecuted and killed? Besides, according to Joel 2:31 and Acts 2:20, the sun, moon, and stars will be darkened *before* the day of the Lord (God's wrath) begins. We do not find this happening until after the 6th seal is broken. So, God's wrath cannot possibly be before the 6th seal.

There is a problem when it is assumed that the tribulation is God's wrath. The tribulation occurs during Satan's wrath. During Satan's wrath (the tribulation/great tribulation), the antichrist will exalt himself and demand worship (2 Thess. 2:4) and only the godly, the saints, or faithful believers will be persecuted (Rev. 12:17). God's wrath brings an end to Satan's wrath and persecution of the saints. Only God will be exalted in the day of the Lord (Is. 2:11, 17) and only the wicked or ungodly will be punished (Is. 13:11; 2 Pet. 3:7). These two events cannot be the same nor can they be going on at the same time. So, the entire tribulation period cannot possibly be God's wrath. Hitchcock and Ice err on this point.

*See chapter four about wrath (All Wrath is Not the Same) for more detail on this subject.

Pre-tribulation Point Eight:

The rapture of the church is imminent or signless.

The pre-tribulationist proclaims that the rapture is imminent. By this they mean that it can happen at any moment without being preceded by any prophetic event. I will list some of the passages that they use to support an imminent rapture (1 Cor. 1:7; 16:22; Phil. 3:20; 4:5; 1 Thess. 1:10; Titus 2:13; Heb. 9:28; James 5:7-9; 1 Pet. 1:13; Jude 1:21; Rev. 3:11; 22:7, 12, 20; 22:17, 20). Because these passages instruct us to *look, watch,* and *wait* for His coming, it is quickly concluded that Christ's return will be signless. Just because we are to look for His return does not mean that it will occur at any moment or that there is nothing left to occur before the rapture.

If you read the previous chapters in this book, you will immediately realize that there are signs associated with Christ's coming (*parousia*) and that the coming of Christ is closely related to (our gathering together) the rapture and the day of the Lord (God's wrath to come). The church will be here until the end of the age (which is the harvest, Matt. 13:38). In Matthew 24, the disciples asked for the sign of Christ coming (*parousia*) and the end of the age (Matt. 24:3). You can read about this in the Matthew 24.

Pre-tribulation Point Nine:

The promise of the 'blessed hope' (Titus 2:13) proves that the rapture will occur 'before' the worldwide tribulation.

In context, these verses associated with the blessed hope read as follows:

> [11] 'For the grace of God that bringeth salvation hath appeared to all men, [12]Teaching us that, denying ungodliness and worldly lusts, we should live soberly,

righteously, and godly, in this present world; [13]*Looking for that blessed hope, and the glorious appearing of the great God and our Saviour Jesus Christ;* [14]Who gave himself for us, that he might redeem us from all iniquity, and purify unto himself a peculiar people, zealous of good works.' (Titus 2:11-14 KJV, emphasis added)

The claim is that the blessed hope cannot be a blessed hope, if the church has to endure great persecution during the tribulation. If any major suffering occurs, the blessed hope would not be comforting. So, the conclusion is drawn that the rapture will occur 'before' the tribulation begins. How one draws this conclusion from Titus 2:13 escapes me. Nevertheless, as Jesus said, 'In the world you will have tribulation; but be of good cheer, I have overcome the world' (John 16:33b NKJV).

The words of Titus are simple. Believers are instructed how to live godly lives on earth until the return of Christ. We should live *godly lives* while here. Living a godly life does come with blessings, but it also comes with a price. We should live with the full understanding that the world will not understand us and will even hate us. What do the Scriptures say about this?

- Jesus said, 'If the world hate you, ye know that it hated me before it hated you.' (John 15:18 KJV)
- 'For unto you it is given in the behalf of Christ, not only to believe on him, but also to suffer for his sake.' (Phil. 1:29 KJV)
- Paul said to Timothy, 'Yea, and all that will live godly in Christ Jesus shall suffer persecution.' (2 Tim. 3:12 KJV)
- 'Confirming the souls of the disciples, and exhorting them to continue in the faith, and that we must through much tribulation enter into the kingdom of God.' (Acts 14:22 KJV)
- 'But if, when ye do well, and suffer for it, ye take it

patiently, this is acceptable with God. [21]For even hereunto were ye called: because Christ also suffered for us, leaving us an example, that ye should follow his steps.' (1 Pet. 2:20b-21 KJV)

- 'Rejoice in hope of the glory of God. [3]And not only *so*, but we glory in tribulations also: knowing that tribulation worketh patience; [4]And patience, experience; and experience, hope.' (Rom. 5:2b-4 KJV)
- [4] 'So that we ourselves glory in you in the churches of God for your patience and faith in all your persecutions and tribulations that ye endure: [5]Which is a manifest token of the righteous judgment of God, that ye may be counted worthy of the kingdom of God, for which ye also suffer.' (2 Thess. 1:4-5 KJV)

In the second chapter of Timothy (verses 1 and 3 NKJV), Paul said, '*Be strong in the grace that is in Christ Jesus... endure hardness, as a good soldier of Jesus.*' The life of a soldier is not always easy. Clearly, we are to be soldiers of Christ. A soldier is expected to endure hardships and to instantly follow the orders of his commanding officer. In combat, a soldier expects to be fired upon. He trains for battle. He does not expect to go home 'before' the battle begins. The battlefield is where the soldier receives his ultimate test. In a war, there will be casualties. Although it is never easy, a well-trained soldier knows and accepts this.

It should be clear that the mere fact that believers are to look for the blessed hope does not exclude them from persecution or tribulation. Yes, believers are excluded from God's wrath, but not the wrath of man through the antichrist. At Christ's coming (*parousia*), the dead in Christ will rise first, and then those who are alive and remain will be caught up with Christ. The comfort is that if you are in Christ, whether dead or alive, you will not miss the blessed hope of His glorious return.

Final Thought

Things are not always as they appear. One night a friend of mine was traveling down a dark highway with her twelve-year old son. As they rounded a curve, they could both see a flashing light in the sky at a distance. It came out of nowhere and seemed to be hovering in the sky. What could this strange light be? Somehow, they were convinced that it was a UFO. Yes, in their minds, this must be a UFO. However, the closer they got, the more they realized that it was not a UFO after all. It was just a radio tower with a flashing light on top. Just as they drew a wrong conclusion in their minds that night, we sometimes draw inaccurate conclusions, because we have not examined an object or a situation close enough. As we have seen with the points discussed in this chapter, sometimes taking a closer look will reveal the truth.

Chapter 10

Will There be a Great Revival after the Rapture?

A s a former pre-tribulationist, I was taught that there would be a great revival after the rapture. It was said that thousands upon thousands of people who were left behind would come to believe in Jesus Christ. They would come to be on fire for the Lord and chose death over denying Christ. The proof text was Revelation 7:9 NKJV, 'After these things I looked, and behold, a great multitude which no one could number, of all nations, tribes, peoples, and tongues, standing before the throne and before the Lamb, clothed with white robes, with palm branches in their hands.' It was said that this great multitude came to believe in Jesus Christ after the rapture of the church. Some said that they were products of the 144,000 Jewish evangelists.

In the *Tim LaHaye Prophecy Study Bible*, notes on Revelation 7:9-14 *a great multitude, which no man could number*, LaHaye says, 'After their sealing and doubtless as a result of their ministry, John sees a multitude from all nations, tongues, and tribes standing 'before the throne, and before the Lamb.' This indicates there will be a great soul harvest during the tribulation that is so enormous it cannot even be counted. Who are these people standing before the throne? John asked that same question, and the angel said, 'These are they who came out of the great tribulation.' The 144,000 witnesses will be so effective during that chaotic time that an innumerable host of people will be saved." [1]

Yet, what drew me to a different conclusion was the comparison of Scripture and attitude of the world toward God, before and after the rapture. In biblically arranging these pieces, an atmosphere of revival is simply not found.

A Powerful Atmosphere of Deception

According to 2 Thessalonians 2:9-11, the antichrist will deceive those who refuse to love the truth and be saved. He will deceive them with powerful signs and lying wonders. In addition to this, God will send a strong delusion so that they will believe the lie and not the truth. All who do not believe will be condemned. With such great deception going on in the world, it simply does not sound like a time of worldwide revival. This deception will occur during the great tribulation (Satan's wrath). This is the very time that the pre-tribulationist reports there will be a worldwide revival. During the great tribulation, we find the entire unbelieving world worshiping Satan (Rev. 13:3-4, 7). Yet, during this same time, those who follow Christ will be persecuted (Rev. 12:17; 13:7). God will even grant the antichrist power to persecute the saints (the elect, believers). In Matthew 24:14, Jesus says that these signs and wonders by the false christs and false prophets will fool all but the elect.

The Unsaved Refuse to Repent

After the rapture occurs, the day of the Lord (God's wrath) will begin. During the day of the Lord, the trumpet and bowl judgments will occur. We find that the *inhabitants of the earth* will refuse to repent for their sins (Rev. 9:20-21 – during the 6th trumpet judgment). They will even blaspheme the name of God

(Rev. 16:9 – during the 4th bowl judgment) and God (Rev. 16:11 – during the 5th bowl judgment and Rev. 16:21 – during the 7th bowl judgment).

Again, Scripture does not paint a picture of great revival during the great tribulation or the day of the Lord. Since it will not be a time of great revival, who are the great multitude mentioned in Revelation 7:9? We will see that the great multitude in heaven is indeed the raptured church; however, they are there after Satan's wrath not before it.

What does this Vital Sign Tell Us?

Throughout this book, we have seen the importance of certain signs described in Scripture concerning the end times. One very important sign is cosmic disturbances (the darkening of the sun, the moon, and the stars) *before* the day of the Lord begins (Joel 2:31). It is clear that a supernatural darkness is associated with the day of the Lord and that the wicked world will be judged at the time of God's wrath (Is.13:9-11; Zeph. 1:14-18). Having said that, according to Scripture, any time that we see the darkening of the sun, moon, and stars in the context of the end times, we should expect the day of the Lord to quickly follow. The day of the Lord (God's wrath) *will not come before* these cosmic disturbances. In the New Testament, it is interesting to note that in the context of the return of Christ, we find cosmic disturbances (Matt. 24:29-31; Mark 13:24-27; Luke 21:25-28; and Rev. 6:12-17). We find that these cosmic disturbances come *after* the tribulation (Matt. 24:29; Mark 13:24). 1 Thessalonians 4:15 teaches that believers will remain on earth until the coming of Christ.

Keep in mind that the tribulation is 'cut short' (Matt. 24:22). This does not mean that the seven-year period (the 70th week of Daniel) will be cut short, but that those who are the object of the persecution in the great tribulation will be removed (thereby ending this persecution). Jesus will be *seen* coming on the clouds at this time (Matt. 24:30; Mark 13:26; Luke 21:27). The angels will be sent to 'gather together the elect.' Matthew 24:31 says the elect will be gathered 'from one end of heaven to the other,' and Mark 13:27 says 'from the farthest part of earth to the farthest part of heaven.' Comparing Matthew and Mark's account we find that they will be gathered from heaven and earth. Luke 21:28 says of the same time that we should look up because our redemption is near. Of course, believers are sealed until the day of redemption (Eph. 4:30).

It All Happens in the Same Day

One thing we should understand is that Jesus spoke of the timing of His return as being like the days of Noah and Lot. What happened during that time? The righteous were rescued and the wicked were destroyed. We saw at the end of Chapter 5 (Matt. 24 – The Olivet Discourse) that the rapture occurs on the same day that the wrath of God begins (Luke 17:26-30). This fact alone should refute the claim that the *great multitude* of people found in heaven in Revelation 7:9 are the product of a worldwide revival caused by the evangelism of the sealed 144,000 Jews. There is simply not enough time. The 144,000 Jews are sealed and the great multitude *suddenly* appears in heaven on the very same day.

At the 6th seal (Rev. 6:12-17) we find the cosmic disturbances, and at the 7th seal (Rev. 8:1-6) we find God's wrath is about to be poured out on the earth. Sandwiched between these two same day events is the sealing of the 144,000 Jews on earth and the appearance of the great multitude in heaven. The pre-tribulationist claims about the 144,000 evangelists simply do not pan out when compared with Scripture and factoring in the timing around these events.

Reading the Vital Sign in the Book of Revelation

Now, let us take the time to put together what we have learned. All the events that occur *before* the divine cosmic disturbances are *not* God's wrath (the day of the Lord). God's wrath will come *after* the tribulation and there will be a gathering of the elect from the farthest part of earth to the farthest part of heaven quickly *after* divine cosmic disturbances. Cosmic disturbances will also occur *before* the elect are redeemed and *before* the day of the Lord begins. Armed with these scriptural facts, let us now look at the timing of cosmic disturbances described in the book of Revelation. We will find it in Revelation 6:12-17. These events occur *after* the sixth seal is broken and *before* the great multitude appear in heaven (Rev. 7:9). Revelation 6:12-17 reads as follows:

> [12] 'I looked when He opened the sixth seal, and behold, there was a great earthquake; and the *sun became black as sackcloth of hair, and the moon became like blood.* [13]*And the stars of heaven fell to the earth, as a fig tree drops its late figs when it is shaken by a mighty wind.* [14]*Then the sky receded as a scroll when it is rolled up, and every mountain and island was moved out of its place.* [15]And the kings of the earth, the great men, the rich men, the commanders, the mighty men, every slave and every free man, hid themselves in the caves and in the rocks of the mountains, [16]and said to the mountains and rocks, 'Fall on us and hide us from the face of Him who sits on the throne and from the wrath of the Lamb! [17]For the great day of His wrath has come, and who is able to stand?' (Revelation 6:12-17 NKJV, emphasis added)

It is clear that cosmic disturbances do not occur until the sixth seal. It is also clear that even the wicked on earth realize that the time for God's wrath, the day of the Lord has come. They tremble with fear over this fact. Now, according to Matthew, Mark, and Luke, we should expect Jesus to be seen coming in the clouds and the elect gathered unto redemption, right? The pre-tribulation view demands that the rapture of the church is imminent. By imminent meaning it is signless and can happen at any moment (even before this sign at the sixth seal). However, scripturally speaking, only *after* cosmic disturbances can the wrath of God and the return of Christ occur. And yes, only after cosmic disturbances can the rapture of the church be *imminent*. It simply cannot occur before that time. So, only *after* cosmic disturbances should we expect a sudden change of the population in heaven.

In Revelation 7:1-8, we find 144,000 children of Israel being sealed on earth. Why are they sealed? God's wrath is about to begin on earth. God does not allow His angels to harm the earth until they are sealed (Rev. 7:3). After this, we find a great multitude in heaven. We find this great multitude in heaven precisely when we would expect the rapture to occur. Revelation 7:9-10, 13-14 reads:

> [9] 'After these things I looked, and behold, *a great multitude which no one could number, of all nations, tribes, peoples, and tongues, standing before the throne and before the Lamb, clothed with white robes, with palm branches in their hands,* [10]and crying out with a loud voice, saying, 'Salvation belongs to our God who sits on the throne, and to the Lamb!'' [13]Then one of the elders answered, saying to me, 'Who are these arrayed in white robes, and where did they come from?' [14]And I said to him, 'Sir, you know.' So he said to me, 'These are the *ones who come out of the great tribulation,* and washed their robes and made them white in the blood of the Lamb.'' (Revelation 7:9-10, 13-14, NKJV, emphasis added)

We find that this great multitude who suddenly appear in heaven have come out of the great tribulation. This is the same time that we should expect the elect to be gathered together. According to Matthew, Mark, and Luke, the elect will be gathered together at the very same time. So it is logical to conclude that this great multitude from Revelation 7:9 and the elect who are gathered from earth and heaven (Matt. 24:31; Mark 13:27) are one in the same. They are the same group. The apostle John had not seen this innumerable group of people in heaven before. They have *just* arrived. This group appears in heaven *before* God's wrath begins, because they are not appointed to God's wrath (1 Thess. 1:10; 5:9; Rom. 5:9).

God's Wrath will not begin before the 5th Seal

Another reason why we know that God's wrath has not occurred before this group appears in heaven is revealed in Revelation 6:9-11. This reason is found in the question asked by the souls who had been slain because of the Word of God and the testimony that they held and the answer that the Lord gave them. This group is found at the fifth seal (Rev. 6:9-11).

> [9] 'When *He opened the fifth seal, I saw under the altar the souls of those who had been slain for the word of God and for the testimony which they held.* [10]And they cried with a loud voice, saying, *'How long, O Lord, holy and true, until You judge and avenge our blood on those who dwell on the earth?'* [11]Then a white robe was given to each of them; and it was said to them that *they should rest a little while longer, until both the number of their fellow servants and their brethren, who would be killed as they were, was completed.'* (Rev. 6:9-11 NKJV, emphasis added)

This passage of Scripture makes it very clear that the previous four seals mentioned in Revelation 6:1-8 (and even the 5th seal) are not the wrath of God. Why do we know this? These faithful souls who had been slain ask the Lord how long it will be before He judges the wicked on earth and avenges their death. In other words, *when* will His wrath begin on earth? God literally tells them that His wrath will not begin until the total number of their fellow servants, which He has determined, are killed (martyred) just like they were. So, we find out two things, God's wrath has not begun and more will be killed before it does begin. Besides, if they had been slain because of God's wrath, why would they ask God to avenge their deaths? It is clear that the ones who would receive judgment are *'those who dwell on the earth.'* People directed by the antichrist are the ones responsible for the death of the martyrs.

We find that *those who dwell on earth* or *the inhabitants of the earth* are hostile to God and His kingdom. The book of Revelation referred to this group of people seven different times. There is nothing positive mentioned about the inhabitants of the earth. This group is in unbelief and will follow the antichrist and the false prophet. The location of the passages and a brief summary of them are as follows:

Those Who Dwell on Earth….

- Revelation 3:10 – (they will be tested)
- Revelation 6:10 – (they will be responsible of the death of the martyrs)
- Revelation 8:13 – (the 3 Woes will be aimed toward them)
- Revelation 11:10 – (they will rejoice over death of the two witnesses)
- Revelation 13:8 – (they will worship Satan)
- Revelation 13:12 – (they will worship antichrist)
- Revelation 13:14 – (they will be deceived by the false signs)

Aligning Events in the Book of Revelation

With all the signs, symbols, figures of speech, the moving back and forth in time, the moving back and forth from scenes in heaven and earth, and other reasons, the book of Revelation can be a very difficult book to understand. The book of Revelation is not only the last book of the New Testament, but it is also the last book of the Bible. So, the better your understanding of the rest of the Old and New Testament books, the better your understanding of the book of Revelation. One of the first things that you must realize is that the book of Revelation is not completely in chronological order, which means that many of the events in the mid to later chapters are going on at the same time earlier chapters (more specifically, parts of chapter 6 – the breaking of some of the seals). The events that are in chronological order are the breaking of the Seven *Seals*, the Seven *Trumpet* Judgments, and Seven *Bowl* Judgments. The *seals* alone take up over 3 ½ years of the 70th week of Daniel.

I have provided a chart to assist you in aligning some of these events. Since this book, *The Rapture Puzzle*, mainly deals with issues surrounding the rapture of the church; the provided chart will only align events that are closely related to the timing of the rapture. The chart should be used to compare events in the book of Revelation with various chapters to reduce confusion and give you somewhat of a time line. The numbers at the left side of the chart will be used as a point of reference moving from top to bottom on the chart. As you look to the right of the numbers you will find specific events mentioned, for example the 4th Seal. To the right of that, you find a brief biblical description of the 4th Seal (Pale Horse/Death/Hades). To the right of the biblical description, you will find the events mentioned in the latter part of the book of Revelation that begin at the same time or go on at the same time as events described at the breaking of the 4th Seal. These events described at the right side of the chart actually give a more detailed description of what is going on during the 4th Seal.

Revelation Chart – Aligning Events

		Revelation - Seals, Trumpets, and Bowls	Revelation - Parallel Events of the Seals, Trumpets, and Bowls
1	1st Seal	White Horse (Antichrist) - Rev. 6:1-2	
2	2nd Seal	Red Horse (Conflict) - Rev. 6:3-4	
3	3rd Seal	Black Horse (Famine) - Rev. 6:5-6	
		**Midpoint of the 70th week of Daniel - The Great Tribulation Begins (3 - 1/2 year point)**	
4	4th Seal	Pale Horse (Death/Hades) - Rev. 6: 7-8	Two witnesses begin ministry - Rev. 11:7-13
			Satan thrown out of Heaven - Rev. 12:7-12
			Everlasting Gospel - Rev. 14:6-11
			Dragon & Beast make war against saints - Rev. 12:17; 13:7 (Wrath of Satan begins - Rev. 13:1-18; 14:1-13)
			False Prophet deceives with signs - Rev. 13:14
			Antichrist – Rev. 13:1-18; False Prophet - Rev. 13:11-17
5	5th Seal	Martyrs (Souls under the altar) - Rev. 6:12-17	
6	6th Seal	Cosmic Disturbances (Darkness) - Rev. 12-17	
6a		144 K sealed - Rev. 7:1-8	
6b		Great Multitude in Heaven Rev. 7:9-17	Earth reaped of believers (Rapture) - Rev. 14:14-16 (*Matt. 13:37-42)
		**The Rapture occurs here (Between the 6th and 7th Seal)**	
7	7th Seal	Reveals that God's wrath/the Day of the Lord is about to begin - Rev. 8:1-6 (*Zeph. 1:7)	
8	1st Trumpet	1/3 of the trees burned - Rev. 8:7	
9	2nd Trumpet	1/3 of the sea destroyed - Rev. 8:8-9	Reaping of those on earth set aside for God's wrath - Rev. 14:14-20
10	3rd Trumpet	1/3 of the rivers made bitter - Rev. 8:10-11	
11	4th Trumpet	1/3 of heavens darkened - Rev. 8:12-13	
12	5th Trumpet	Locust torment men for five months - Rev. 9:1-12	
13	6th Trumpet	1/3 of mankind is killed - Rev. 9:13-21	
14	7th Trumpet	Kingdoms of the world become Christ's - Rev. 11:15-19	
		**70th week of Daniel Ends (7-year period ends)**	
15	1st Bowl	Loathsome Sores on those with mark - Rev. 16:2	
16	2nd Bowl	The Sea turns to blood - Rev. 16:3	
17	3rd Bowl	The Waters turn to blood - Rev. 16:4-7	
18	4th Bowl	Men are scorched by the sun - Rev. 16:8-9	
19	5th Bowl	Darkness and pain - Rev. 16:10-11	
20	6th Bowl	Great River Euphrates dries up - Rev. 16:12-16	
21	7th Bowl	Earthquakes and great hail fall - Rev. 16:17-21	

Chapter 11

The End Times View of the Early Church Fathers

Some have said that what is now called the pre-wrath view of the rapture (what I consider the biblical view) is a new view. However, it is not a new view. If you look back at what the early church fathers (from the second and third century) believed and wrote, you would see that their words did not line up with the teaching of the pre-tribulation rapture view of today. We will look at quotes from at least five orthodox Ante-Nicene (before the Council of Nicea in 325 AD) church fathers. These well-known and respected men are the Pastor of Hermes, Justin Martyr, Irenaeus, Hippolytus, and Tertullian.

The Pastor of Hermes (40 – 140AD): The Pastor of Hermes was also called 'The Shepherd of Hermes.' Clement of Alexander, Origen, and Irenaeus had the opinion that some of his writings should be viewed as Scripture. Even though it was rejected as Scripture, it continued to be recommended reading for new converts. The Pastor of Hermes did not hold the pre-tribulation rapture view.

'Happy ye who endure the great tribulation that is coming.' (Vision Second)

'Those, therefore, who continue steadfast, and are put through the fire, will be purified by means of it... Wherefore cease not speaking these things into the ears of the saints. This then is the type of the great tribulation that is yet to come.' (Vision Fourth)

Justin Martyr (100 – 165AD): Justin Martyr was an early Christian writer. He (Justin) taught Christian philosophy at Ephesus. He left in 135 AD for Rome where he taught and wrote until he was martyred under the Roman Emperor Marcus Aurleius. Two of Justin's works are *Apology* and *Dialogue with Tryho.* Justin's own words revealed that he believed the church would have to endure the persecution of the antichrist. In other words, he did not hold the pre-tribulation rapture view.

'The man of apostasy (Antichrist)... shall venture to do unlawful deeds on the earth against us the Christians.' (Justin Martyr, *Tryho cx*)

Irenaeus (175 – 195AD): Irenaeus, the Bishop of Lyons in southern France, was one of the most important Christian writers of the second century. He studied under Polycarp (an early Christian martyr, 70 – 156AD), who was a student of John (the apostle and disciple of Jesus). Irenaeus was the first to state the four gospels (Matthew, Mark, Luke, and John) as canon (Scripture) and was also the first to write as a theologian of the church. His primary work was *Against Heresies.* He clearly did not hold a pre-tribulation rapture view.

'And they (the ten kings)... shall give their kingdom to the beast, and put the Church to flight.' (Irenaeus, *Against Heresies* 5.26.1)

Hippolytus (160 – 236AD): Hippolytus was a theologian. He was the most important theologian of the Roman church in the third century and the first that we have writing of who wrote a commentary on the book of Daniel. Hippolytus was a student of Irenaeus. As already mentioned, Irenaeus was a student of Polycarp, who was a student of John, who was a student of Jesus. As seen in the writings of Hippolytus, he fully expected the church to be on earth during the persecution of the antichrist.

> '*Now concerning the tribulation of the persecution which is to fall upon the Church from the adversary (the Antichrist and his persecution of the saints)... That refers to the one thousand two hundred and threescore days (the last half of Daniel's seventieth week) during which the tyrant is to reign and persecute the Church.*' (Hippolytus, *Treatise on Christ Antichrist*, pp. 60, 61)

Tertullian (160 – 225AD): Tertullian is credited with being the author of such sayings as 'The blood of the martyrs is the seed of the Church,' 'See how they (Christians) love one another,' 'If God will,' 'God bless,' and 'God grant.' If you have heard these, you have heard Tertullian's work. His work had a great effect on the later church fathers and even on the Council of Nicea (325 AD). It is believed that Tertullian was the first to use the Latin word *trinitas (trinity)* as a term to describe the Godhead (Deity, as three persons in one substance). But what did Tertullian have to say about the end times?

> '*That the beast Antichrist with his false prophet may wage war on the Church of God... Since, then, the Scriptures both indicate the stages of the last times, and concentrate the harvest of the Christian hope in the very end of the world.*' (Tertullian, *On the Resurrection of the Flesh*, xxv; cf *Scorpiace*, xii)

Tertullian makes it clear that the church would remain on earth through the persecution of the antichrist and that the harvest (rapture) would occur at the end of the age. These five early church fathers are not the only ones who held this view. There are many others who held this view, and there are none that I know of during this time that refute this view. These Ante-Nicene church fathers *did not* hold the pre-tribulation view.

The Didache (Teaching of the Twelve Apostles) (70 – 140AD): The Didache was a document respected by some of the church fathers as being next to the Holy Scripture. One of its purposes was to keep the church pure. Those who were preparing for baptism and church membership used it. It also contained a summary of basic instructions about Christian life. The last chapter was on eschatology and even gave a sequence of events on the end times.

> '*For in the last days false prophets and corrupters shall be multiplied... and then shall appear the world-deceiver as Son of God, and shall do signs and wonders, and the earth shall be delivered into his hands, and he shall do iniquitous things which have never yet come to pass since the beginning... And then shall appear the signs of the truth; first, the sign of an outspreading in heaven; then, the sound of the trumpet; and the third, the resurrection of the dead; yet not of all, but as it is said: Then shall the world see the Lord coming upon the clouds of heaven.*'
> (*The Didache (Teaching of the Twelve Apostles)*)

What are We to Believe?

It is clear that these early church fathers stood between the first century believers and us today. They believed that there would be a future time of persecution for the followers of Christ (the true church). They fully realized the horrors that the believers in the first century had to endure; yet they understood that more persecution was ahead for the church. The church would face the antichrist. The church would not be taken away before persecution from the antichrist began. They were expecting wrath from this man of lawlessness.

Throughout this book, careful comparisons were made. Scripture was compared with Scripture. Now it is up to you to decide. Do you believe that the church will be removed before any persecution? Or do you now believe that those who follow Christ and desire to live godly will suffer persecution – yes, persecution at the hands of the antichrist?

I heard someone say, if pre-tribulation is right, pre-wrath is no problem, but if pre-wrath is right, pre-tribulation *is a problem*. If you are a believer, are you prepared to remain faithful to the end, even if you will have to pay for it with your very life? Remember that eternal life awaits you on the other side. Death has no control over you. It is merely a doorway on to an eternal life that is free from suffering, pain, and tears. As a fellow believer, I encourage you to remain faithful to the end of your life or until the return of Christ.

Jesus said in Revelation 22:12-13 KJV, 'And, behold, I come quickly; and my reward *is* with me, to give every man according as his work shall be. I am Alpha and Omega, the beginning and the end, the first and the last.' In the words of the apostle John, (Rev. 22:20b-21 NKJV) 'Even so, come, Lord Jesus! The grace of our Lord Jesus Christ *be* with you all. Amen.'

Chapter 12

The Jewish Fall Feasts Point to End-Times Events

G od gave to Israel seven special feasts that celebrated and looked forward to the coming of the Messiah, the redemption of His people, and future fulfillment of prophecy. They were literally rehearsals for what was to come. These Feasts of the LORD have much to do with prophecy. It is unfortunate that many of the body of believers do not understand the great significance of these feasts. I feel that shedding light on these feasts will assist us in our understanding of prophecy. There are also a couple of good books to read on this subject. One, *The Feasts of the LORD*, by Kevin Howard and Marvin Rosenthal and the other is *God's Appointed Times*, by Barney Kasdam.

The main purpose for this chapter is to bring insight to the significances of the final three feasts of the LORD and reveal their fulfillment in the book of Revelation. After thinking long and hard on how this chapter should be written, I decided to make a chart and explain its contents. The chart will show the future fulfillment of the remaining three feasts of Israel. It will also reveal their approximate timing in reference to the major prophetic events in the book of Revelation. The chart will also show which Scriptures are related and which overlap within the book of Revelation. I must emphasize that *no way* in this chapter am I predicting *dates* or *when* the event will happen, only an approximation of *where* they fit on the time line related to the seals, trumpets, and bowls within the book of Revelation.

There are seven feasts. You may already know that seven is a number of completeness in Scripture. Each feast is a literal rehearsal for the nation of Israel for an actual event to come in the future. The first four are spring feasts and have already been fulfilled. They are as follows:

1. *Passover* (which speaks of *redemption* and the Passover Lamb [Jesus Christ] who was slain for us).
   (Lev. 23:5; John 11:55-57; 13:1)
2. *Unleavened Bread* (which speaks of *sanctification*, it began the day after Passover and was fulfilled when Jesus' body laid in the grave and did not see decay).
   (Lev. 23:6; Acts 2:31, 32; 13:37)
3. *Firstfruits* (which speaks of Christ's *resurrection*, Firstfruits was fulfilled when Jesus rose bodily from the grave).
   (Lev. 23:9-14; 1 Cor. 15:20-23)
4. *Weeks or Pentecost* (which speaks of *origination*, the coming of the Holy Spirit was fulfilled with the birth of the church through the New Covenant).
   (Lev. 23:15-16; Acts 2:1-4)

Each of these first four feasts has already been fulfilled and are connected with Christ's first coming. All four of them were fulfilled on the very day that they were celebrated. All seven of the feasts looked to a prophetic event in the future. The details and Jewish traditions that surround these feasts are amazing. However, they (the first four feasts) are not the focus of this chapter.

The last three are fall feasts and have yet to be fulfilled. They each occur in the Jewish month of Tishri, which falls in the month of September or October. These feasts are connected with Christ's yet future second coming (*parousia*). They are as follows:

5. *The Feast of Trumpets/Rosh Hashanah* (which occurs on the 1st of Tishri)
6. *The Day of Atonement/Yom Kippur* (which occurs on the 10th of Tishri).
7. *The Feast of Tabernacles/Sukkot* (which occurs on the 15th of Tishri).

Making Comparisons of Feasts, Events, and the Book of Revelation

As mentioned in chapter 10, the book of Revelation is not only the last book of the New Testament, but it is also the last book of the Bible. It will not only fulfill the prophecies of the New Testament, but it will also fulfill long awaited prophecies of the Old Testament as well. So, the better your understanding of the rest of the Old and New Testament books, the better your understanding of the book of Revelation. One of the first things that you must realize is that the book of Revelation is not completely in chronological order. For example, details surrounding the 4th seal in the 6th chapter of Revelation are found in parts of chapters 11, 12, 13, and 14 of the book of Revelation. As you can imagine, this adds to the confusion associated with the book. However, the chart that I have provided will assist you in understanding the order of events. The chart should be used to compare events in the book of Revelation with various chapters to reduce confusion and give you somewhat of a timeline. It will also compare the events of Revelation with the Jewish Feast that have yet to be fulfilled. The background of these Jewish Feasts will be explained. The numbers at the left side of the chart are a point of reference and will be used throughout this chapter. The following bullets will give a brief outline of numbers 1 through 7 on the chart.

- Numbers 1 through 3 (Seals 1, 2, and 3) on the chart occur during a time which Jesus called the 'Beginning of Sorrows' (Matt. 24:8) and will end when the Great Tribulation begins. This will start at the beginning of what most call the tribulation period (the 70th week of Daniel).

- Number 3a marks the approximate midpoint of the 70th week of Daniel.

- Number 4 on the chart (the 4th Seal) shows when the Great Tribulation begins. Events in chapters 11, 12, 13, and 14 of Revelation are occurring at the same time as number 4.

- Number 5 (the 5th Seal) is a result of the events in number 4.

- Number 6 (the 6th Seal) reveals darkness. The Feast of Trumpets is observed during a time when the night sky is at its darkest. This will be explained in this chapter. According to the book of Joel, there will be darkness before the day of the Lord (Joel 2:30-31).

- Numbers 6a and 6b reveal protection and deliverance, protection for the 144,000 Jews and deliverance for those who trusted in Christ during the Great Tribulation. This deliverance is the rapture. I believe that the rapture is revealed in the reaping of believers in Revelation 14:14-16, which is also described in Matthew 13:37-42. They are removed before God's wrath (the Day of the Lord) begins. This will cut short the Great Tribulation (number 6c).

- Number 7 (the 7th Seal) is a solemn pause before the day of the Lord begins. This is also supported by Zephaniah 1:7.

Jewish Feast Fulfillment in the Book of Revelation

	Revelation	Parallel Revelation Events	Jewish Feast Fulfillment
1	1st Seal - White Horse (Antichrist) – Rev. 6:1-2		
2	2nd Seal - Red Horse (Conflict) – Rev. 6:3-4		
3	3rd Seal - Black House (Famine) – Rev. 6:5-6		
3a	Midpoint of 70th week of Daniel (3 - 1/2 years) - The Great Tribulation is about to begin - The elect (faith believers) will be persecuted (Matt. 24:21)		
4	4th Seal - Pale Horse (Death/Hades) – Rev. 6:7-8	Two witnesses begin their ministry – Rev. 11:7-13	
		Satan is thrown out of Heaven – Rev. 12:7-12	
		Everlasting Gospel – Rev. 14:6-11	
		The Dragon & Beast make war against the saints – Rev. 12:17; 13:7; (The wrath of Satan begins – Rev. 13:1-18; 14:1-13)	
		False Prophet deceives with signs – Rev. 13:14	
		Antichrist – Rev. 13:1-8; False Prophet – Rev. 13:11-17	
5	5th Seal - Martyrs (Souls under the altar) – Rev. 12-17		
6	6th Seal - Cosmic Disturbances (Darkness) – Rev. 6:12-17		Darkness precedes the Day of the Lord (The Feast of Trumpets is celebrated during a dark evening sky)
6a	144K sealed – Rev. 7:1-8		
6b	Great Multitude in Heaven – Rev. 7:9-17	Earth Reaped of believers (Rapture) – Rev. 14:14-16 (*Matt. 13:37-42)	
6c	The Great Tribulation (Satan's wrath) is cut short by Christ's coming & rapture -- Matt. 24:22,29-31; Mark 13:20 - God's wrath (the Day of the Lord) is about to begin		
7	7th Seal - Reveals that God's wrath/the Day of the Lord is about to begin – Rev. 8:1-6 (*Zeph. 1:7)		
8	1st Trumpet (1/3 of tree burned) – Rev. 8:7		
9	2nd Trumpet (1/3 of sea destroyed) – Rev. 8:8-9		
10	3rd Trumpet - (1/3 of rivers made bitter) – Rev. 8:10-11	Reaping of those on earth set aside for God's wrath – Rev. 14:17-20	Feast of Trumpets (Rosh Hashanah), which precedes the Day of Atonement (The time between the Feast of Trumpets and the Day of Atonement is called the "The Days of Awe")
11	4th Trumpet - (1/3 of heavens darkened) – Rev. 8:12-13		
12	5th Trumpet - (Locust torment men) – Rev. 9:1-12		
13	6th Trumpet - (1/3 of mankind killed) – Rev. 9:13-21		
14	7th Trumpet - (Kingdom becomes Christ's) – Rev. 11:15-19	The Ark of the Covenant is seen in heaven – Rev. 11:19 (The ark was only seen on the Day of Atonement)	The Day of Atonement (Yom Kippur) begins at the 7th trumpet
15	*The 70th week of Daniel ends approximately here (7 years) / The two witnesses are killed & resurrected 3 - 1/2 days later – Rev. 11:7-14		
16	Seven Bowl Judgments – Rev. 16:1-21	Armageddon-Antichrist & False Prophet destroyed – Rev. 19:20	
17	Millennial (1000 yr) Kingdom - Christ Reigns on Earth – Rev. 20:4		The Feast of Tabernacles (Sukkot)

The Two Witnesses in Revelation 11
(Number 3a and 4 on the chart)

The ministry of the two witnesses will last for 1260 days. We saw back in chapter 3 'Daniel's Time Line of the End Times' that 1260 days; 42 months; and a time, times, and half a time all refer to the *last* 3 ½ years of the 70th week of Daniel. So, this would place the ministry of the two witnesses from the midpoint of the 70th week of Daniel to the end of it. Although we find the two witnesses in chapter 11 of the book of Revelation, their ministry actually begins back in the chapter 6, somewhere between the 3rd and 4th seal (at the abomination of desolation).

At the end of the testimony of the two witnesses, they will be killed, their dead bodies will lie in the streets for three and a half days, and their enemies will celebrate; however, after three and a half days, the two witnesses will come to life and ascend into heaven (Rev. 11:7-14). The 7th trumpet will then sound. The 7th trumpet is sounded at the end of the 70th week of Daniel. The 7th trumpet also brings us to the end of the fulfillments of the Feasts of Trumpets. Trumpet blasts precede the Day of Atonement (Yom Kippur).

The Feast of Trumpets (Rosh Hashanah)
(Numbers 8 through 13 on the chart)

This section will describe the background of the Feast of Trumpets. Numbers 8 through 13 on the chart reveal the fulfillment of the Feast of Trumpets. The Feast of Trumpets is also called Rosh Hashanah. Rosh Hashanah is Hebrew and literally means *Head of the Year*. Although it is not known by this name in Scripture, its roots are from the Bible. It is called a 'Memorial of Blowing of Trumpets' (Lev. 23:24) and a 'Day of Blowing the Trumpets' (Num. 29:1). Based on these biblical descriptions, Rosh Hashanah was simply called 'the Feast of the Trumpets.' This was of course a day of sounding trumpets. It was celebrated on the first day of the seventh month (Lev. 23:24;

Num. 29:1), which is the Hebrew month Tishri (Sept.-Oct.). You might ask, 'If it is celebrated on the first day of the seventh month, how can it be at the head of the year?' Good question. I will be glad to explain. You see biblically the Jews used two kinds of calendars: the *Civil Calendar* (an official calendar for kings, childbirth, and contracts) and the *Sacred Calendar* (from which the festivals were computed). So Tishri is the 1st month of the year on the civil calendar and the 7th month of the year on the sacred calendar. Six months after Tishri is the month of Nisan (March-April) and is the 7th month of the civil year and the 1st month of the sacred year.

New Moon equals New Month

You may have noticed that the Jewish months do not correspond exactly to our months. For example, a Jewish month may begin in mid-July and end in mid-August. I can explain. The Jewish months are lunar (having to do with the moon). The moon orbits the earth in approximately 29 ½ days. In these 29 ½ days the moon passes through the different phases (new, half, full). The number of days in a Jewish month usually alternate from 29 to 30 days each month (of course averaging 29 ½ days per month). Each new month (or new moon) is based on a new thin crescent appearing at the edge of the moon. The rest of the moon is dark at this time. This is called the new moon. The Jewish calendar is so closely related to the new moon that the Hebrew word for moon (*chodesh*) is also the word for *month*. The night sky is noticeably darkened at this time. Throughout Scripture, a darkened moon and sun (cosmic disturbance) is given as a 'sign' that the Day of the Lord is near (Joel 2:31). It is also a sign that Christ's second coming (Matt. 24:29-31), the redemption of the saints (Luke 21:25-28) and the wrath of God (Rev. 6:12-17) is near. The Feast of the Trumpets is the only feast that is celebrated while the sky is naturally dark. However, the sky will be divinely darkened at its future prophetic fulfillment.

Reasons for Trumpet Blowing

There are two main reasons for the blowing of the trumpet in Scripture. The first is the *calling of the assembly / gathering God's people together* (Num. 10:1-2) and the second reason is *to go to war* (Num. 10:9). Prophetically, the last trump that Paul speaks of is one of gathering God's people. This is known as the rapture of the church. It will be a gathering of both the dead in Christ (the resurrection) and of those in Christ who are alive and survive the persecution of the antichrist (1 Cor. 15:51-52; 1 Thess. 4:16-17). It also looks to the glorious appearance of our Lord and Savior Jesus Christ (Matt. 24:30-31) who will deliver us from the wrath to come (1 Thess. 1:10) because the church is not appointed to the wrath of God (1 Thess. 5:9; Rom. 5:9).

In the book of Revelation, we read of seven trumpets that are associated with the wrath of God. The first six trumpet blasts are found in chapters 8:7 through chapter 9, and the 7th trumpet blast is found in chapter 11:15-19. During this time, God makes war with the earth. 'The Lord alone will be exalted in that day' (Is. 2:17).

An ancient Jewish tradition says that the resurrection of the dead would occur on Rosh Hashanah. The gravestones of many Jews are engraved with a *shofar* (trumpet). From the words of Paul and our Lord Jesus Christ, we see in Scripture that the trumpet sound is closely associated with the resurrection of the righteous and the rapture (1 Cor. 15:51-52; 1 Thess. 4:16-17; and Matt. 24:30-31).

Divine Darkness (A 'Sign' that the Day of the Lord is near) (Number 6 on the chart)

The Feast of the Trumpets will be the next feast on the Lord's agenda to be fulfilled. As said before, this feast is celebrated while the night sky is naturally darkened by the lack of light being reflected from the moon, which of course is associated with the day of the Lord. Yet, Scripture speaks of this time as being a time of divine darkness. There is a great deal said in Scripture about the eschatological day of the Lord. By eschatological, I mean the final day of the Lord. The prophets spoke of it as a time of great darkness, destruction, and the coming of God's wrath upon the earth at the end of this age. Here are some verses about the day of the Lord and the darkness associated with it.

> [14] 'The great day of the LORD *is* near, *it is* near, and hasteth greatly, *even* the voice of the day of the LORD: the mighty man shall cry there bitterly. [15]*That day is a day of wrath, a day of trouble and distress, a day of wasteness and desolation, a day of darkness and gloominess, a day of clouds and thick darkness,* [16]*A day of the trumpet and alarm against the fenced cities,* and against the high towers.' (Zeph. 1:14-16 KJV, emphasis added)

> [9] 'Behold, the day of the LORD cometh, cruel both with wrath and fierce anger, to lay the land desolate: and he shall destroy the sinners thereof out of it. [10]For the *stars of heaven and the constellations thereof shall not give their light: the sun shall be darkened in his going forth, and the moon shall not cause her light to shine.* [11]And I will punish the world for *their* evil, and the wicked for their iniquity; and I will cause the arrogancy of the proud to cease, and will lay low the haughtiness of the terrible.' (Is. 13:9-11 KJV, emphasis added)

We have seen over and over again that the moon and the sky will be divinely darkened at this time (Joel 2:31; 3:15; Is. 13:9-10; 34:4, 8; Acts 2:20). We have also seen that this will be a time when God pours out wrath upon the earth and the nation of Israel. Israel is warned in Scripture not to look forward to the day of the Lord. For those who are left on earth (the unbelieving nation of Israel and the enemies of God), it will be a time of God's wrath and judgment.

> [18] 'Woe unto you that desire the day of the LORD! to what end is it for you? the day of the LORD is darkness,

and not light. [19]As if a man did flee from a lion, and a bear met him; or went into the house, and leaned his hand on the wall, and a serpent bit him. [20]Shall not the day of the LORD be darkness, and not light? Even very dark, and no brightness in it?' (Amos 5:18-20 KJV)

There is no doubt that darkness precedes the day of the Lord (Joel 2:31). The Day of the Lord is also associated with trumpet blasts. According to Christ in Matthew 24:29, Mark 13:24, and Luke 21:25, divine darkness will occur before His return. It causes the wicked to tremble with fear, and reveals that the time of redemption for the followers of Christ is near. We find the earth divinely darkened in the book of Revelation at the opening of the 6th seal.

[12] 'I looked when He opened the sixth seal, and behold, there was a great earthquake; and the *sun became black as sackcloth of hair, and the moon became like blood.* [13]*And the stars of heaven fell to the earth, as a fig tree drops its late figs when it is shaken by a mighty wind.* [14]Then the sky receded as a scroll when it is rolled up, and every mountain and island was moved out of its place. [15]And the kings of the earth, the great men, the rich men, the commanders, the mighty men, every slave and every free man, hid themselves in the caves and in the rocks of the mountains, [16]and said to the mountains and rocks, 'Fall on us and hide us from the face of Him who sits on the throne and from the wrath of the Lamb! [17]For the great day of His wrath has come, and who is able to stand?'' (Rev. 6:12-17 NKJV, emphasis added)

There is a two-fold purpose for this time. One is for God to bring judgment on His enemies and the enemies of the saints (2 Thess. 1:6-8) and the other is to bring the nation of Israel to repentance (Zech. 12:10; Dan. 12:24).

The Days of Awe
(Numbers 8 through 13 on the chart)

The theme of the Feast of Trumpets (Rosh Hashanah) is repentance. There are ten days between Rosh Hashanah and Yom Kippur (the feast that follows Rosh Hashanah). Jewish tradition says that the ten-day period between Rosh Hashanah and Yom Kippur are called the 'Days of Awe.' It is believed that will be the last chance to repent before God's final judgment. It is a time for the people of Israel to examine themselves. They will have to take a look at their spiritual condition and make necessary changes in their lives. Jewish tradition says that three books are opened on Rosh Hashanah (which also looks forward to the day of the Lord): the *Book of Life for the Righteous,* the *Book of Life for the Wicked,* and the *Book of Life for the In-between.* Those whose names are written in the book of the righteous will live a prosperous life in the coming year. Those whose names are written in the book of the wicked will have their lives cut short in the year to come. (Their judgment is final and no other chance for repentance will be granted.) The others (the book of the in-between) will have a chance to repent before Yom Kippur (the Day of Atonement). Those who truly repent will live to see the following year.

Although the tradition of these books do not line up with Scripture, the thought does come from Scripture. It comes from the words of David, 'Let them be blotted out of *the book of the living,* and not be written with the righteous.' (Ps. 69:28 NKJV) and from the words of Moses, 'Yet now, if thou wilt forgive their sin—; and if not, blot me, I pray thee, out of thy book which thou hast written. And the LORD said unto Moses, Whosoever hath sinned against me, him will *I blot out of my book*' (Ex. 32:32-33 KJV emphasis added).

Since repentance is the main focus of Rosh Hashanah (prophetically, the Day of the Lord), the *shofar* (ram's horn) is sounded to alert the people that the time for repentance is near. We also find this to be so in Scripture. Trumpet blasts occur during the day of the Lord (Joel 2:1, 15; Zeph. 1:16; Zech. 9:14; Rev. 8 & 9).

The 7 trumpets in the book of Revelation reflect the theme of repentance and the Days of Awe. We have seen that cosmic disturbances precede the day of the Lord. Scripture says that a time of silence also precedes this period of time.

> [7] *'Be silent in the presence of the Lord GOD;* For the day of the LORD is at hand, For the LORD has prepared a sacrifice; He has invited His guests.' (Zeph. 1:7 NKJV, emphasis added)

> [1] 'When He opened the seventh seal, there was *silence in heaven for about half an hour.* [2]And I saw the seven angels who stand before God, and to them were given seven trumpets.' (Revelation 8:1-2 NKJV, emphasis added)

Just in case you are wondering what all of these Jewish traditions surrounding Rosh Hashanah have to do with the rapture and the day of the Lord, I will briefly explain. There are two major reasons for trumpets to be blown in Scripture (gathering God people and a call to war; Num. 10:1-2, 9). The next trumpet blast on God's timetable is the call of God's people to His presence (the rapture). This will be the call for those faithful followers (saints) of Christ. The dead in Christ will be resurrected with new bodies and the living will be changed. The darkness of the cosmic disturbances will precede this as a sign that the day of the LORD (God's wrath) is about to begin and the resurrection of the dead in Christ is about to occur.

The Days of Awe point to the days between the beginning of God's wrath and the end of the 70th week of Daniel. These are the days of divine judgment on the world for the wicked and a time to bring the nation of Israel to repentance. At the end of this period, some on earth will have repented and others will not. Aligning Jewish tradition with this outcome would be to say that those who repented would be those in the *Book of Life for the Righteous;* those who do not repent would be those in the *Book of Life for the Wicked,* and those in the *Book of Life for the In-between* would be for those who could go either way. So their destination would be unknown until the end of the day of the LORD.

The Day of Atonement (Yom Kippur)
(Number 14 on the chart)

Yom Kippur or the Day of Atonement is Israel's most solemn and holy day of all. Yom Kippur and Rosh Hashanah are specifically religious holidays. *Yom Kippur* literally means *day of covering or Day of Atonement*. This was a divinely instituted day when the sins of the nation of Israel for the previous year were covered. Historically, the Holy of Holies (a place in the temple that housed the Ark of the Covenant) was entered only one day of the year. That was on the Day of Atonement. On this day, the high priest would enter the Holy of Holies to atone for the sins of the nation. The Day of Atonement was to be observed on the 10th of Tishri (Lev. 23:27), between the Rosh Hashanah/Feast of Trumpets [1st of Tishri] and the Sukkot/Feast of Tabernacle [15th of Tishri].

Our Lord and Savior Jesus Christ fulfilled and finished the work that the Day of Atonement looked forward to. Yet, Israel as a nation has not believed and received Jesus' finished work on the cross. I have provided a chart that compares the historical Day of Atonement with how Jesus fulfilled it in His life and ministry.

Overview and Fulfillment of the Day of Atonement in Christ	
Day of Atonement	**Fulfillment of Day of Atonement in Christ**
The high priest wore regular priestly garments that day (Lev. 16:4)	Jesus came to the earth in the form of a bondservant (John 1:14; Phil. 2:6-8)
The high priest alone performed the sacrifice to make atonement (Lev. 16:14-15)	Jesus humbled himself and became obedient to death on the cross (Phil. 2:8)
The high priest had to be ritually clean to carry out the service (Num. 19:1-10)	Jesus perfectly fulfilled the law and lived a sinless life (Heb. 9:14)
The blood of animals was used to atone for sins (Heb. 9:7, 22)	Christ used His own blood to obtain our eternal redemption (Heb. 9:11-14) and took away the sins of the world (John 1:29)
The sacrifices were without blemish (Num. 29:8)	Jesus did not sin; therefore, He was without blemish (2 Cor. 5:21; Heb. 4:15)
The high priest entered the Holy of Holies (made with hands) only on this day (Lev. 16:34; Heb. 9:7)	Jesus entered the Holy of Holies made without hands – the Holy of Holies in heaven (Heb. 4:14; 9:11-12)
The nation of Israel was not to do any work on that day; anyone who did would be killed/destroyed by God (Lev. 23:30-31)	We cannot work for our salvation; all who try to work for salvation will die in their sins (Gal. 2:16; Eph. 2:8-9; John 8:24)
This was a solemn day of rest (Lev. 23:32)	All who trust in Christ are to rest in the finished work of Christ on the cross (Eph. 1:13-14; 2:8-9)

Prophetically, the Day of Atonement (for the nation of Israel) looks to the end of the 70th week of Daniel (the last seven-year period of prophecy) when Israel finally receives Jesus as their Messiah. According to Leviticus 23:27, the Day of Atonement was to be a day of mourning. The nation was to afflict their souls. On the future fulfillment of this day for the nation of Israel, they will finally see Jesus as their long-awaited Messiah. This will occur at the 7th trumpet blast.

'And I will pour upon the house of David, and upon the inhabitants of Jerusalem, the spirit of grace and of supplications: and they shall look upon me whom they have pierced, and they shall mourn for him, as one mourneth for *his* only *son*, and shall be in bitterness for him, as one that is in bitterness for *his* firstborn.' (Zech. 12:10 KJV)

At last, Israel's Day of Atonement will be fulfilled for them and God will remember their sins no more.

²⁴ 'Seventy weeks are determined upon thy people and upon thy holy city, to finish the transgression, and *to make an end of sins*, and to make reconciliation for iniquity, and to bring in everlasting righteousness, and to seal up the vision and prophecy, and to anoint the most Holy.' (Dan. 9:24 KJV, emphasis added)

²⁵ 'I, even I, am he that *blotteth out thy transgressions* for mine own sake, and will not remember thy sins.' (Is. 43:25 KJV, emphasis added)

³⁴ 'And they shall teach no more every man his neighbour, and every man his brother, saying, Know the LORD: for they shall all know me, from the least of them unto the greatest of them, saith the LORD: for I will *forgive their iniquity, and I will remember their sin no more.*' (Jer. 31:34 KJV, emphasis added)

Earlier we said that the Day of Atonement was the only day of the year that the Holy of Holies was entered. This means that day was the only time that the Ark of the Covenant was seen. Only on the nation of Israel's day of repentance was it seen. The earthly Ark of the Covenant has not been seen since 586BC, when the Babylonians destroyed Solomon's Temple. Some say that it was hidden under the temple mount, others that it was destroyed, and even others that it was sent to Ethiopia. It makes no difference, because the ark was merely a copy of what is in heaven. (Heb. 9:23-24)

[24] 'For Christ has not entered the holy places made with hands, which are copies of the true, but into heaven itself, now to appear in the presence of God for us.' (Heb. 9:24, NKJV)

It is interesting to note that after the seventh trumpet is sounded in chapter eleven of the book of Revelation, the temple of God is opened in heaven and the Ark of the Covenant is seen in His temple (Rev. 11:19). This could only mean that Israel's Day of Atonement has finally come.

[19] 'And the temple of God was opened in heaven, and there was seen in his temple the ark of his testament: and there were lightnings, and voices, and thunderings, and an earthquake, and great hail.' (Rev. 11:19 KJV)

A 30-Day Mourning Period
(Numbers 16 on the chart)

The fulfillment of the Day of Atonement (Yom Kippur) for Israel will come at the end of the 70th week of Daniel. Israel will accept Jesus as their Messiah. The days preceding it are called the days of Awe, which of course is during the day of the Lord, also called God's wrath. The Day of Atonement is a day of mourning for Israel.

We find a 30-day mourning period to be consistent with the Old Testament. The nation mourned 30 days for Aaron after his death (Num. 20:29) and also 30 days for Moses after his death (Deut. 34:8). There will be a future 30-day mourning period for Israel. However, this future mourning period will occur when the nation of Israel realizes that Jesus is their long-awaited Messiah. Zechariah 12:10 NKJV says, 'And I will pour on the house of David and on the inhabitants of Jerusalem the Spirit of grace and supplication; then they will look on Me whom they pierced. Yes, they will mourn for Him as one mourns for his only son, and grieve for Him as one grieves for a firstborn.' The nation of Israel will mourn when they see that Jesus is the Messiah. This 30-day period is immediately after the 70th week of Daniel, which some call the tribulation period. Daniel 12:11 NKJV says, 'And from the time that the daily sacrifice is taken away, and the abomination of desolation is set up, there shall be one thousand two hundred and ninety days.' In this verse, we see 30 days added on to the 1260-day period, which is the final 3 ½-year period of the week of Daniel. This 30-day period of mourning for Israel will fall between the 70th week of Daniel and the beginning of the millennial kingdom. During this 30-day period, the seven bowl judgments will be poured out on earth.

BEGINNING OF SORROWS	WRATH OF SATAN	God's Wrath	God's
Matt. 24:8	GREAT TRIBULATION	THE LORD OF THE LORD	Wrath
	Matt. 24:21		
3 - 1/2 YEARS - 1260 DAYS	3 - 1/2 YEARS - 1260 DAYS	30	45
70TH WEEK OF DANIEL - 7 YEAR PERIOD		DAYS	DAYS
	1260 + 30 = 1290 DAYS - Dan. 12:11		
	1260 + 30 + 45 = 1335 DAYS - Dan. 12:12		

PRE-WRATH RAPTURE

The Feast of Tabernacles (Sukkot)
(Number 17 on the chart)

The final feast to be fulfilled in the future is the Feast of

Tabernacles (or Sukkot). It will be fulfilled during the millennial kingdom. *Tabernacle* comes from the Latin word *tabernaculum*, meaning *a hut, a booth, or a temporary shelter*. The word *Sukkot* is the plural word for *sukka* and is the Hebrew word equivalent to *hut or booth*. The Feast of Tabernacles is also known in Scripture as the Feast of Ingathering (Ex. 23:16; 34:22). It was called the Feast of Ingathering because it was celebrated after all the crops had been harvested and gathered for the year. The biblical roots of this feast are found in Leviticus 23:33-43. It is celebrated on the 15th of Tishri and the celebration lasts for seven days (Lev. 23:34). The first and the eighth day are considered holy convocations, sacred assemblies, or Sabbaths, no customary work was done on those days.

All natives of Israel were to dwell in booths made of citron trees (a lemon-like fruit), leafy trees (myrtle type), palm branches, and willows for seven days (Lev. 23:39-42). This celebration looked back at God's provision for the nation of Israel during its 40-year stay in the wilderness after leaving Egypt. This was a celebration of great joy. The joy was for the present provisions and the future provisions.

The Water-Drawing Ceremony

There where two major highlights of the feast. The first was the Water-Libation Ceremony – a sacrificial water-pouring ceremony. This ceremony looked to the anticipation of rain. Just after dawn each morning the high priest would carry a golden pitcher from the temple to the Pool of Siloam (which was just south of the city of Jerusalem in Jesus' day). A joyous procession of worshipers would follow the high priest as he made his way to the Pool of Siloam. After filling the pitcher with water from the pool, the joyful procession made their way back to the temple. At that time the priest would say, 'Therefore with joy you will draw water from the wells of salvation' (Is. 12:3 NKJV).

The high priest walked around the altar once and made his way up the altar, held the golden pitcher of water up and poured it to the ground. This was a visual prayer for rain. He did this for seven days. On the seventh and final day, he walked around the altar seven times (the last day of the feast was considered the great or greatest day [John 7:37]). At the proper time during each morning's ceremony, the procession, waving palm branches would sing Psalm 118:25 NKJV, 'Save now, I pray, O LORD; O LORD, I pray, send now prosperity.' Psalm 118 is considered a Messianic psalm. You may recall that during Jesus' triumphal entry into Jerusalem, the crowd waved palm branches and shouted "Hosanna!' (which means *save now*) Blessed is He who comes in the name of the LORD!' (Matt. 21:8, 9; Luke 19:38; John 12:13) Although, not a direct quotation, it is reminiscence of Psalm 118:25-26. This happened on the Sunday Jesus rode into Jerusalem during the triumphal entry; today it is called Palm Sunday. It is interesting to note that the great multitude standing before the throne (Rev. 7:9-10 NKJV) hold palm branches and cry out, 'Salvation belongs to our God who sits on the throne, and to the Lamb.'

The Temple-Lighting Ceremony

At night during the Feast of Tabernacles, the Temple-Lighting ceremony was held. This was held from the second night through the final night of the feast. Four menorahs (lampstands), probably several stories high, stood in the court of the women. It was the younger priest's job to climb ladders and fill the menorahs with olive oil. The light from the menorahs lit the temple area and city of Jerusalem. It was reminiscent of the shekinah glory (Ezekiel 43:1-6). All through the night, the Sanhedrin (a group of 71 leaders in Israel) would perform torch dances.

This ceremony preceded the Water-Drawing ceremony. It was said that nothing in ancient Israel compared to this ceremony. In so many words, it was said that you have not seen joy until you have seen the water-drawing.

Water, Light, Tabernacle, and Christ in the Book of John

As you can imagine, after this seven-day and seven-night celebration of great joy, the images of the water drawing and light ceremony would be clearly in the minds and hearts of Israel. With this in mind, think about the words of Christ from the gospel of John. The events of John 7:1-10:21 occurred during the Feast of Tabernacles, with John 7:37 - 10:21 covering only two days.

Water

With all the pageantry of the final day of the Water-Drawing ceremony, including the high priest circling the altar seven times and pouring water from a golden pitcher, Jesus makes a bold statement.

> [37] 'On the last day, that great *day* of the feast, Jesus stood and cried out, saying, *'If anyone thirsts, let him come to Me and drink.* [38]*He who believes in Me, as the Scripture has said, out of his heart will flow rivers of living water.'* [39]But this He spoke concerning the Spirit, whom those believing in Him would receive; for the Holy Spirit was not yet *given,* because Jesus was not yet glorified.' (John 7:37-39 NKJV, emphasis added)

As you can imagine, a statement like this at this time would cause many reactions. You will find immediate reactions in verses 40 through 53 in the seventh chapter of John. Of course, this claim could only come from Christ, the Messiah.

Light

The day following the last day of the Feast of Tabernacles was considered a Sabbath (Lev. 23:39; John 9:14). Again, keep in mind the people had just celebrated with joy the Temple-Lighting

Ceremony each night for the past week. Early that very morning, the scribes and Pharisees brought a woman caught in adultery before Jesus. This famous story is recorded in John 8:1-11. Consider the impact of Jesus' following statement to the listeners recorded in verse 12.

'Then Jesus spoke to them again, saying, '*I am the light of the world. He who follows Me shall not walk in darkness, but have the light of life.*'' (John 8:12 NKJV, emphasis added)

Before this statement, Jesus told the woman to 'go and sin no more.' He was literally saying, 'You have now seen the true light, not only from the temple, but Me. You should now turn from darkness (sin) to light – a life pleasing to God that you will find in Me.'

Later Jesus performs a miracle that was unheard of. He healed a man blind from birth. Before doing this, Jesus said to His disciples. '*As long as I am in the world, I am the light of the world.*' (John 9:5 NKJV, emphasis added) The following happened after this statement.

[6] 'When He had said these things, He spat on the ground and made clay with the saliva; and He anointed the eyes of the blind man with the clay. [7]And He said to him, 'Go, wash in the pool of Siloam' (which is translated, Sent). So he went and washed, and came back seeing. [8]Therefore the neighbors and those who previously had seen that he was blind said, 'Is not this he who sat and begged?' [9]Some said, 'This is he.' Others *said*, 'He is like him.' He said, 'I am *he*.' [10]Therefore they said to him, 'How were your eyes opened?' [11]He answered and said, 'A Man called Jesus made clay and anointed my eyes and said to me, 'Go to the pool of Siloam and wash.' So I went and washed, and I received sight.'' (John 9:6-11 NKJV)

Here we have a man who lived in darkness all of his life. After coming face to face with the light of the world, he received sight. Did you notice that the man was sent to wash in the Pool of Siloam? This was the very place that the high priest collected water from for the water drawing ceremony.

Tabernacle

John 1:14 NKJV says, 'And the *Word* became flesh and *dwelt* among us, and we beheld His glory, the glory as of the only begotten of the Father, full of grace and truth.' The word for *dwelt* literally means *tabernacle*. The Word of God literally tabernacled with us. Revelation 19:13 also identifies Jesus as the Word. (He *was* clothed with a robe dipped in blood, and His name is called The Word of God.) He dwelled temporally in flesh with us. Of course, during the Feast of Tabernacles, the Israelites temporally dwelled in booths.

Future Fulfillment of the Feast of Tabernacles (Number 17 on the chart)

The book of Revelation reveals the fulfillment of the Feast of Tabernacles. In it, we also see the fulfillment of Jesus' claim to be the water and light.

Water

[6] 'And He said to me, 'It is done! I am the Alpha and the Omega, the Beginning and the End. *I will give of the fountain of the water of life freely to him who thirsts.*'' (Rev. 21:6 NKJV, emphasis added)

[1] '*And he showed me a pure river of water of life, clear as crystal, proceeding from the throne of God and of the Lamb.*' (Rev. 22:1 NKJV, emphasis added)

[17] 'And the Spirit and the bride say, 'Come!' And let him who hears say, 'Come!' *And let him who thirsts come. Whoever desires, let him take the water of life freely.*' (Rev. 22:17 NKJV, emphasis added)

Light

[23] 'The city had no need of the sun or of the moon to shine in it, for the *glory of God illuminated it. The Lamb is its light.*' (Rev. 21:23 NKJV, emphasis added)

[5] 'There shall be no night there: They need no lamp nor light of the sun, *for the Lord God gives them light.* And they shall reign forever and ever.' (Rev.22:5 NKJV, emphasis added)

Tabernacle

[1] 'Now I saw a new heaven and a new earth, for the first heaven and the first earth had passed away. Also there was no more sea. [2]Then I, John, saw the holy city, New Jerusalem, coming down out of heaven from God, prepared as a bride adorned for her husband. [3]And I heard a loud voice from heaven saying, '*Behold, the tabernacle of God is with men, and He will dwell with them, and they shall be His people.* God Himself will be with them and be their God.'' (Rev. 21:1-3 NKJV, emphasis added)

[22] 'But I saw no temple in it, for *the Lord God Almighty and the Lamb are its temple.*' (Rev. 21:22 NKJV, emphasis added)

Final Thought

This chapter alone could make an enlightening and informative

Bible study. I remember my time in U.S. Marine Corps boot camp at Parris Island in early 1981. We were told that everything we learned to do (down to the smallest detail) was for a reason. The closer we got to graduation day, the more it became apparent that this was true. Nothing we learned was without reason. It all tied together in the end. With the significances of all the Jewish feasts along with the many traditions, it is clear that God has a future plan for Israel. The eternal God of the universe does nothing by chance.

God is Preparing Us for Such a Time

I f you previously thought that the church would be removed from earth before the antichrist appears, the Scriptural teaching of this book could be somewhat of a shock to you. It is not my intent to offend or frighten anyone with this book. However, it is my intent to reveal Scriptural truth. Truth can sometimes be difficult to accept. Nevertheless, just the thought of having to endure persecution or tribulation can bring extreme anxiety or fear to many. None of us knows specifically all that the future holds for us. I suppose that is a good thing. Our Lord gives us enough grace for each day. He is always preparing us for tomorrow; all the while molding and renewing minds to be more like Christ's. This takes time.

God gives us strength when we need it. The Lord has strengthened me time and time again. If and when the time comes, those of us who are weak will be made strong. This is because it will not be us, but it will be the Holy Spirit controlling us in a super-natural way as only the Lord can do. Most of us probably do not feel worthy enough to be called by God for some great work. You might say, 'what great work could I possibly do for God?' Well, just like the rest of us, in and of yourself you can do nothing.

When we are weak, God is strong. God is in the business of calling ordinary people to do great and marvelous works for Him. You my friends, are no different than the great men and women of Scripture. God prepared each and every one of them to do a great work for Him. If called upon, are *you* ready today to face the antichrist and be a light for Christ? It does not matter, allow God to prepare you day by day. If an occasion as such does arise, it will not be you speaking, but the Holy Spirit. In a moment of weakness, Peter denied Jesus three times. Yet, when filled with the Holy Spirit, Peter boldly preached and 3000 were saved that day. Praise be to God for that. Who knows if you will be a Peter or an Esther? Just be obedient and allow God to work in your life. He will handle the rest. May the grace of our Lord and Savior Jesus Christ be with you all.

How to Use the End-Times Chart

This chart is used to make comparisons with the same prophetic events described in different biblical books. This chart starts at the top with the beginning of the 70th week of Daniel and covers the major events all the way through to the Great White Throne Judgment. Comparisons are made with the books of Revelation, Matthew, Mark, Luke, Thessalonians, and Daniel. These books are listed in columns at the top of the chart with their content below.

Below the listing of each book are biblical references in that specific book. The references begin with the beginning of the 70th week of Daniel and work their way down to the Great White Judgment (if the specific book covers events that far). As you work your way down the chart, look to the left and or right to compare specific events mentioned in that book with the same event as it is described in another book. This will assist you in getting a clear picture of end-time events as well as their approximate timing.

END-TIMES CHART - COMPARING SCRIPTURE WITH SCRIPTURE
(This chart compares the same prophetic events described in different books of the Bible)

REVELATION	MATTHEW, MARK, & LUKE	THESSALONIANS	DANIEL
70th Week of Daniel begins here (7 year period) - The first 3-1/2 years are "the beginning of sorrows" – Matt. 24:8			
1st Seal *Antichrist – Rev. 6:1-2	False christs – Matt. 24:5; Mk. 13:8		Antichrist confirms covenant (Begins 70th week) – Dan. 9:27a
2nd Seal *Conflict/Wars (Red Horse) – Rev. 6:3-4	Wars/Rumors – Matt. 24:6, 7a; Mk. 13:7; Lk. 21:9		
3rd Seal *Famine (Black Horse) – Rev. 6:5-6	Famine – Matt. 24:7; Mk. 13:8; Lk. 21:11a		
Middle of the 70th Week of Daniel, approximately here (3-1/2 years/42 months) Covers thru the first 3 seals			
Great Tribulation (Satan wrath) is about to begin / The elect (faithful believers) will be persecuted – Matt. 24:21			
Two witness begin ministry - lasting 1260 days (Rev 11:3) which ends just before the 7th trumpet (11:7-13)			
4th Seal *Death/Hades (Pale Horse) – Rev. 6:7-8	Death – Matt. 24:9; Mk. 13:12; Lk. 21:16		
Satan thrown out of Heaven – Rev. 12:7-12		Restrainer stops restraining – 2 Thess. 2:2:5-6	Michael Stands still – Dan. 12:1 "Time of trouble" – Dan. 12:1b
Everlasting Gospel – Rev. 14:6-11	Gospel of the Kingdom – Matt. 24:14		
Dragon & Beast make war against saints – Rev. 12:17; 13:7 (Wrath of Satan begins – Rev 13:1-18; 14:1-13)	Abomination of desolation – Great Tribulation begins – Matt. 24:15,21; Mk. 13:14,19	Man of Sin (Antichrist) exalts himself – 2 Thess. 2:4; Apostasy – 2 Thess. 2:3	Antichrist exalts himself - Dan 11:36, Abomination of Desolation (Middle of the Week) – Dan. 9:27b
Betrayal & love grows cold – Matt. 24:10,12; Mk. 13:9,11a; Lk. 21:16			
False Prophet deceives with signs – Rev. 13:14; Antichrist – Rev. 13:1-8; False Prophet – Rev. 13:11-17	Great signs deceive – Matt. 24:24; Mk. 13:22	Lying wonders – 2 Thess. 2:11	
5th Seal *Martyrs/Souls under altar – Rev. 6:9-11	Martyrdom – Matt. 24:9,10		
Cosmic Disturbances "before" the Day of the LORD – Joel 2:31; Acts 2:20			
6th Seal *Cosmic Disturbances – Rev. 6:12-17	Cosmic Disturbances – Matt. 24:29; Mk. 13:24-26; Lk. 21:16		
144K Sealed on Earth – Rev. 7:1-8			
Great Multitude in Heaven (Rapture) Rev. 7:9-17; Earth Harvested – Rev. 14:14-16	Christ Coming "Parousia" (Rapture) Matt. 24:29-31; Mk. 13:24-27; Lk. 21:25-28	Believers "caught up" (Rapture) – 1 Thess. 4:15-17	"Many awaken to everlasting life" – Dan. 12:2a
The End of the Age - Harvest is the end of the age – Matt. 13:39, Jesus with believers until the end of the age – Matt. 28:20			
Great Tribulation (Satan's wrath) is "Cut short" by Christ's Coming "Parousia" & Rapture (Matt. 24:22,29-31; Mk. 13:20)			
7th Seal *God's wrath (the Day of the LORD) about to begin – Rev. 8:1-6 (Silence in heaven – Zeph. 1:7)			
THE DAY OF THE LORD (The wrath of God) Begins "The LORD alone is exalted" (Is. 2:11,17)			
7 Trumpet Judgment – Rev. 8:7-21; 11:15-19			
Two witness killed & resurrected 3 1/2 days later (Rev. 11:7-14)			
World becomes Christ's – Rev. 11:15	*70th Week of Daniel ends approx. here (7 yrs)*		Israel Saved – Dan. 9:24
7 Bowls Judgments – Rev. 16:1-21			
Armageddon-Antichrist & False Prophet destroyed – Rev. 19:20			Abominator Desolate – Dan. 12:11
(The Wrath of God is complete) 7 BOWLS LAST 30 DAYS – Dan. 12:11 (1260 + 30 = 1290 Days)			
45 Days Until Millennial Kingdom begins – Dan. 12:12 (1260 + 30 + 45 = 1335 Days)			
Beginning of Christ's Reigns (New Heaven & Earth) – Isaiah 65:17-25			
CHRIST REIGNS ON EARTH - Millennial (1000 yr) Kingdom – Rev. 20:4			
Great White Throne Judgment (All at this judgment are lost) – Rev. 20:11-25			Lost awaken to shame & everlasting contempt – Dan. 12:2b

Glossary
End-Time Definitions

This glossary will assist you in understanding key end-time terms used in the context of Scripture and this book. The definitions are somewhat brief. Some will differ in one degree or another from other end-time views, yet you will find that they are accurate according to Scripture.

1260 Days (see *time, times, and half a time*)

It is the same period of time as 42 months, time, times, and half a time, and 3 ½ years.

144,000, the

The 144,000 are 12,000 Jews from each of the twelve tribes (excluding Ephraim and Dan). They are described as servants of God who are sealed on their forehead after the darkening of the sun, moon, and stars, but before the wrath of God is initiated (Rev. 7:1-8). This 144,000 Jews do not worship the antichrist or take on his mark during the great tribulation. God protects them on earth during His time of wrath (the day of the Lord). This special group is also described as being the firstfruits of God and the Lamb (Christ) having no deceit and without fault (Rev. 14:1-5). It is unclear exactly when they became believers in Christ – at the time they are sealed (during the rapture) or at the end of the 70th week of Daniel. *Some* describe the 144,000 as witnesses who evangelize

Jewish Babies

the earth and bring many to Christ; however, Scripture does not describe them in this way.

42 months (see *time, times, and half a time*)
It is the same period of time as 1260 days; time, times, and half a time; and 3 ½ years.

Abomination of Desolation, the
An abomination is that which is detestable to God, such as idolatry. Specifically the abomination of desolation referred to the desecration of the temple. It was desolated by Antiochus Epiphanes in 168BC and will be desolated in the future by the antichrist. The antichrist will sit in the temple of God and demand worship at the midpoint of the 70th week of Daniel.

Antichrist
He will oppose Christians, Jews, and anyone who won't obey him. He will exalt himself to be worshipped. He will be a world leader who will ultimately persecute all who do not submit to his rule (Israel and the followers of Christ) during a time called the great tribulation. He is also referred to in Scripture as the son of perdition, the man of sin, the beast, and other names.

Apostasy, the
The Greek word for apostasy literally means a defection from the truth. '*The* apostasy' is specifically referred to in 2 Thessalonians 2:3 as 'the falling away.' This will occur before Christ's coming and the rapture. In the Olivet Discourse, Jesus speaks of this time as a time when 'they will deliver you up to tribulation and kill you, and you will be hated by all nations for My name's sake. And then many will be *offended (scandalize, entice to sin, or apostatize),* will betray one another, and will hate one another.' (Matthew 24:9-10 NKJV, emphasis added)

Armageddon, the Battle of
It is the final military confrontation on the earth before the millennium (Rev. 19:11-21). The *seventh trumpet* initiates the

bowl judgments and the Battle of Armageddon, which begin after the 70th week of Daniel. The antichrist and his armies of the earth will gather to make war against Christ and His army. Christ will destroy the armies of the earth. The antichrist and the false prophet will then be cast alive into the lake of fire burning with brimstone. Satan will then be bound and cast into the bottomless pit for a thousand years.

Beginning of Sorrows, the
Referred to by Jesus as a time before the end of the age, when false christs, wars, rumors of wars, and famine with occur. These things will occur before the end of the age. It is the first 3 ½ years of the 70th week of Daniel (Matt. 24:4-8; Rev. 6:1-6). Jesus said that we should not be troubled during this time (Matt. 24:6).

Bondservant
A faithful, dedicated follower of Christ.

Bowl Judgments
The *bowl judgments* are the final judgments of the book of Revelation dealing with the wrath of God. They begin after the 70th week of Daniel. The *bowl judgments* last for 30 days and are initiated by the seventh trumpet. It will culminate at the Battle of Armageddon. It will complete God's wrath on the wicked world. (Rev. 15:1 through 16:21)

Days of Awe, the
In Jewish tradition, these are the 10 days between the Feast of Trumpets (a time of repentance) and Yom Kippur (the Day of Atonement). It is believed that this is a last chance to repent before God's final judgment. (Also see chapter on Jewish Feasts.)

Day of the Lord (the wrath of God)
The most prophesied event in the Old Testament, it will be a time of God's fiery judgment of the wicked on earth (God's wrath). It is also called the 'end of the age.' It is associated with the final harvest and the seventh seal. The Day of the Lord will

begin at the coming of Christ when the faithful are rescued. It cuts short the great tribulation for the believers in Christ. After Christ's coming, God's wrath will begin, the wicked will be destroyed, and the kingdom of darkness (Satan's kingdom) will be brought to an end. This time of judgment will begin at the seventh seal. It will include the trumpet and bowl judgments and culminate at the Battle of Armageddon. Divine darkness (darkening of the sun, moon, and stars) and worldwide earthquakes will precede the Day of the Lord. The entire world will see this sign and the wicked world will realize that God's wrath is about to begin. (Joel 2:1-11; 2:30-32; Is. 2:11-21; Is. 13:6-11)

Elect
In the most general sense, it represents all true believers, past, present, and future. They make up the Kingdom of God.

End of the Age, the (see *Day of the Lord*)
It is a New Testament term for the day of the Lord. There will be a harvest of people at the end of the age. (Matt. 13:36-43)

Eschatology
It is the biblical study of prophecy and end-time events surrounding it.

False Prophet, the
He will be a false prophet of the antichrist. The false prophet will perform great signs in the presence of antichrist and deceive the unbelieving world. He will require all to worship the image of the antichrist and receive his mark. All who do not worship the image will be killed, that is, all who can be caught (Rev. 13:11-18). After the Battle of Armageddon, the false prophet along with the antichrist will be cast alive into the lake of fire (Rev. 19:20).

Great Tribulation, the (see *Satan's wrath*)

God's Wrath, the wrath of God (see the *Day of the Lord*)

Gospel of the Kingdom
It should not be confused with the gospel of Christ. The gospel of the kingdom is a call for repentance and a warning of divine judgment for those who refuse. This gospel was preached by John the Baptist and Jesus. It will also be preached be an angel during the end times. (Matt. 3:1-12; Matt. 24:14; Rev. 14:6-7)

Last Day, the
This is the day when the church is raptured (see *Rapture*). The resurrection of the dead in Christ will occur on the *Last Day*. It initiates the end of the age and begins the day of the Lord, which occur on the same day.

Last Days
It is a period of time associated with prophetic events prior to the rapture of the church.

Mid-tribulation Rapture View
The mid-tribulation rapture view holds that the rapture of the church will occur at the midpoint of the 70th week of Daniel, when the abomination of desolation occurs.

Midpoint of 70th week
The antichrist will desecrate the temple at this time. This will begin the great tribulation. After he desecrates the temple, he will begin his persecution of the elect of God and those of the nation of Israel who refuse to submit to his rule.

Millennium, the
This is a thousand-year period of time after the 70th week of Daniel, when Christ will rule God's kingdom on earth. This will be a time of great peace and is described in Isaiah 65:17-25 This specific thousand-year time period is referred to in Revelation 20:1-10. Satan will be bound during this time, but released for a short time after this period (Rev. 20:1-3). He'll then be cast into the lake of fire and brimstone (Rev. 20:7-10). Some hold that this will be a literal 1000-year period of time and others do not.

Olivet Discourse, the

Refers to Jesus' teaching on the end times, given to the disciples while sitting on the Mount of Olives. It is recorded in Matthew 24 and 25, Mark 13, and some parts are located in Luke 21.

Persecution

This word comes from a Greek word that means *pressure* and is translated as *tribulation*. Although those who have trusted is the Lord throughout history have been persecuted as many are today, there will be a time of great persecution in the future that has not been equal to in all of history. It is referred to as the 'great tribulation' when the nation of Israel and followers of Christ are persecuted by the antichrist during the wrath of Satan. This persecution will be cut-short by the return of Christ. It should not be confused with the wrath of God (the day of the Lord), when God will judge the wicked on earth, which comes after the return of Christ.

Post-tribulation Rapture View

The view holds that Christ will return after the 70th week of Daniel and that the church will be protected through God's wrath.

Pre-tribulation Rapture View

The view holds that Christ's return is imminent (can happen at any moment) and needs no other prophetic signs to be fulfilled. It also holds that the entire 70th week of Daniel is God's wrath and that the church will be raptured from earth sometime before the 70th week of Daniel begins.

Pre-Wrath Rapture View

The view holds that the true church will be raptured during the great tribulation (persecution) of the antichrist. It also holds that the rapture will occur after the midpoint of the 70th week of Daniel, but before God's wrath (the day of the Lord) begins. It holds that the midpoint begins Satan's wrath (the great tribulation), not the wrath of God. It also holds that signs are associated with the return of Christ.

Prophetic Year

This is the way that Scripture calculates a year when referring to prophetic events. A prophetic year is a 360-day period of time.

Rapture, the

It is the gathering together of true believers (the elect) to Christ in the clouds at His second coming. No one knows the exact day, but it will occur sometime between the middle and the end of the 70th week of Daniel. It will occur between the sixth and the seven seal of the book of Revelation, sometime during the persecution of the elect on earth (during the great tribulation). The *Rapture* will cut short the great tribulation by removing the object of the antichrist's persecution. The resurrection of the dead in Christ will also occur at the *Rapture*. The *Rapture* will occur at the end of the age and will initiate the day of the Lord (God's wrath).

Saints

The Greek word literally means *holy ones* or *sacred*. They are separate from the rest of the world and consecrated to God. They are the ones who believe in Jesus Christ. Their lifestyle reflects their confession of faith. They are described as those who name Jesus as Lord, and they are also called the faithful and true witnesses of Jesus Christ.

Satan's Wrath (the wrath of Satan)

This is a time on earth when Satan uses the antichrist to persecute the nation of Israel and the true church. This time is called 'the great tribulation' when only the righteous are persecuted on earth. It begins at the halfway point of the 70th week of Daniel when the abomination of desolation occurs. However, Satan's wrath will be cut-short at the return of Christ. Satan's wrath should *not* be confused with God's wrath (the day of the Lord). During the God's wrath, only the wicked are persecuted.

Seven Seals of Revelation, the

The *first three seals* occur at the beginning of the 70th week of Daniel. Jesus referred to this time as the beginning of sorrows. The *fourth seal* initiates the 3 ½-year point of the 70th week of Daniel, when the abomination of desolation and the great tribulation begin. The *sixth seal* initiates the sign of the day of the Lord (end of the age). The *seventh seal* initiates the trumpet judgments, God's divine wrath on the wicked world (the day of the Lord). The breaking of the seals is recorded in Revelation 6:1-17; 8:1-6. Much of what occurs during the breaking of the seals can be paralleled with events described by Jesus in Matthew 24:4-8, 15-22.

Seventh Seal

It is the final seal broken on the scroll described in the book of Revelation. It begins God's wrath (the day of the Lord), which includes the seven trumpet and seven bowl judgments, when God will judge the wicked inhabitants of the earth. (Also see the *Day of the Lord.*)

Seventieth Week of Daniel

It is the final seven-year period of prophecy to be fulfilled on earth. During this time, events such as the beginning of sorrows, the great tribulation (Satan's wrath), the rapture of the church, the resurrection of the dead in Christ, and the day of the Lord (God's wrath) will occur.

Sign of Christ's coming, the

This sign will immediately follow the sign of the end of the age. The sign of Christ's coming will be the supernatural light of Christ's great glory as Christ descends into the earth's atmosphere in the clouds. It will be a time when God's *shekinah* glory will be seen throughout the world. It will come out of great darkness (the sign of the end of the age). Everyone will see it. Christ will come in the clouds and gather together His elect. (Matt. 24:30; Mark 13:26; Luke 21:27; Rev. 1:7)

Sign of the End of the Age, the

It is a time of divine darkness (darkening of the sun, moon, and stars) and worldwide earthquakes. It precedes the coming of Christ and the day of the Lord. The wicked world will tremble with great fear at the sign of the end of the age. (Joel 2:31-32; Matt. 24:29; Mark 13:24-25; Rev. 6:12-17; Is. 2:10, 19)

Three and a half years (see *time, times, and half a time*)

Time, times, and half a time

It refers to the last 3 ½-year period of the 70th week of Daniel. A 'time' means one year. 'Times' means two years and 'a half a time' means a half of a year. Add them together and you get 3 ½ years. Time, times, and half a time, 42-months, 1260 days all refer to the same period of time, which is also called the second half of the 70th week of Daniel.

Tribulation (great tribulation, the wrath of Satan)

It will be a time of great persecution for those who believe in Christ (when the elect are persecuted for their faith in Jesus Christ) or for those who refuse to worship the antichrist. It is a time of Satan's wrath. The wicked world will not be persecuted during this time. The antichrist will exalt himself above all and demand worship or allegiance. The tribulation/great tribulation precedes the coming of Christ. This should *not* be confused with the day of the Lord or God's wrath when God judges the wicked on earth. It's also called 'the time of Jacob's trouble' (Jer. 30:7) and 'a time of trouble such as never was.' (Dan. 12:1, see also Matt. 24:9-10, 21, 29; 2 Thess. 2:3-4)

Trumpet Judgments

There are seven *trumpet judgments* in the book of Revelation. They occur during the day of the Lord when God's wrath is poured out on the wicked world. The trumpet judgments are after the seals, but before the bowl judgments. The *trumpet judgments* begin after the rapture of the church. The first *six trumpets* will occur some time during the second half of the 70th week of Daniel and go up to the end of this seven-year period. The *seventh trumpet* will be sounded after the little scroll is opened. The *seventh trumpet* initiates the bowl judgments and the Battle of Armageddon, which begin after the 70th week of Daniel. Prior to the *seventh trumpet*,

God removes the spiritual blinders off the surviving remnant of Israel, and they will come to the knowledge of Jesus Christ. (Rev. 8:7-9:21; Rev.10:1-11; Rev. 11:15-19; Dan. 12:11)

Witnesses, the Two

They prophesy for 1260 days (3 ½ years; 42-months) clothed in sackcloth (Rev. 11:3), during the second half of the 70th week of Daniel (beginning at the start of the great tribulation). Although a good argument can be made that they are Moses and Elijah (and they very well could be), Scripture does not actually call them by those names. Two of several reasons why most call them Moses and Elijah are because the miracles they perform during their 3 ½-year ministry resemble the miracles of these two Old Testament prophets (Rev. 11:5-6; Exodus 7-11; 1 Kings 17), also their appearance together with Christ on the Mount of Transfiguration (Matt. 17:1-13). They are described as the two olive trees and lampstands standing before God on earth (Rev. 11:4). God will allow them to be killed when their testimony is finished (at the end of the 70th week of Daniel); however, they will be resurrected after 3 ½ days and ascend to heaven (Rev. 11:7-12).

Greek and Hebrew Words with Strong's Number

(The words are listed in the order they first appear in this book.)

Thlipsis, #2347, pressure, persecution, or trouble
Megas, #3173, large, strong, or great
Erchomai, #2064, to come or to go
Parousia. #3952, a presence or presence with
Katargeo. #2673, reduced to inactivity
Aion, #165, an age or era
Odin, #5604, a pang or throe, childbirth pain
Skandalizo, #4624, to entrap or entice to sin, apostasy or displeasure; to make to offend
Apostasia, #646, defection or revolt, a defection from the truth
Hupomeno, #5278, to stay or remain under, to bear trials or have fortitude, persevere
Sothesetai, #4982, save or deliver
Euaggelion. #2098, a good message, gospel
Koloboo. #2856, to amputate or shorten
Episunago. #1996, to collect upon

Ouranos, #3772, sky or heaven

Oros, #3735, a mountain, hill, or mount

Parabole, #3580, a placing beside, to case or throw beside, parable

Manthano, #3129, to learn by inquiry or observation

Airo, #142, to take up or away or remove

Paralambano, #3880, to receive near or to associate with

Aphiemi, #863, to send forth, leave, lay aside, omit, remit, suffer

Gregoreuo, #1127, to keep awake, be vigilant, be watchful

Perileipo, #4035, survive (or leave around)

Harpazo, #726, to seize, snatch or catch away

Soteria, #4991, rescue, deliverance

Chazaq, #2388, bind, conquer, or restrains (*Hebrew word*)

Amad #5975, to stand (*Hebrew word*)

Katargeo, #2673, to reduce to inactivity or render useless

Tereo, #5083, to guard or protect from loss (Keep)

Hupomone, #5281, endurance, continue to wait patiently (Persevere)

Ek, #1537, out of (From)

Peirasmos, #3986, a putting to proof by testing or tempting, temptation (Trial)

Hoti, #3748, because (Because)

Peirazo, #3985, test, scrutinize, entice, examine, or prove (Tempt)

Hagios, #40, consecrated, separated

Episunagooge, #1997, collection

Chodesh, #2320, month (*Hebrew word*)

Endnotes

Chapter 5

[1] W. E. Vine, Merrill F. Unger, and William White, Jr., *Vine's Expository Dictionary of Old and New Testament Words*, (Chattanooga, Tennessee: AMG Publishers, 1996) 111.

Chapter 6

[1] 'Revised Standard Version of the Bible, Apocrypha, copyright 1957; The Third and Fourth Books of the Maccabees and Psalm 151, copyright 1977 by the Division of Christian Education of the National Council of the Churches of Christ in the United States of America.

[2] Ibid.

Chapter 7

[1] Jay P. Green, ed., *Interlinear Greek/English New Testament* third ed., 4th printing, (Grand Rapids: Baker Books, 2001) 630.

[2] A Marvin Rosenthal seminar

Chapter 8

[1] Marvin R. Vincent, *Vincent's Word Studies* Vol 2., 'The Writings of John,' Electronic Edition, (Hiawatha, Iowa: Parsons Technology, 1998.)

Chapter 9

[1] Mark Hitchcock and Thomas Ice, *The Truth Behind Left Behind: A Biblical View of the End Times*, (Sisters, Oregon: Multnomah, 2004) 33.

Chapter 10

[1] Tim LaHaye, Edward Hindson, Thomas Ice, and James Combs, eds. *Tim LaHaye Prophecy Study Bible*, (Chattanooga, Tennessee: AMG Publishers, Inc., 2000) 1376.

Bibliography

Anderson, Sir Robert. *The Coming Prince.* Grand Rapids: Kregel Classics, reprinted 1957.

Cooper, Charles. *Defining the Prewrath Rapture.* Video. The Sign Ministries, 2000.

Cooper, Charles. *Pursuing Truth: An Introduction to Bible Interpretation.* DVD. Sola Scriptura, Pre-wrath Institute. 2004.

Green. Jay P., ed. *Interlinear Greek/English New Testament.* Third ed., 4th printing. Grand Rapids: Baker Books, 2001.

Hitchcock, Mark., and Thomas Ice. *The Truth Behind Left Behind: A Biblical View of the End Times.* Sisters, Oregon: Multnomah, 2004.

Howard, Kevin., and Marvin Rosenthal. *The Feasts of the LORD.* Nashville: Thomas Nelson, 1997.

Howard, Kevin. *God's Appointed Times.* Baltimore: Lederer Books, 1993.

LaHaye, Tim, Edward Hindson, Thomas Ice, and James Combs, eds. *Tim LaHaye Prophecy Study Bible.* Chattanooga,

Tennessee: AMG Publishers, Inc., 2000.

Rosenthal, Marvin. *The Pre-Wrath Rapture of the Church.* Nashville: Thomas Nelson, 1990.

Strong, James, Dr. Warren Baker, ed. *Strong's Complete Word Study Concordance, Expanded Edition.* Chattanooga, Tennessee: AMG Publishers, 2004.

Sproul, R.C. *Knowing Scripture.* Downers Grove, Illinois: Intervarsity Press, 1977.

Van Kampen, Robert., and Charles Cooper. *Understanding Scripture at Face Value* Grand Haven, Michigan: Sola Scriptura, 1999.

Van Kampen, Robert. *The Sign.* Wheaton: Crossway Books, 1992.

Vincent, Marvin R. *Vincent's Word Studies.* Vol. 2., 'The Writings of John,' Electronic Edition, Hiawatha, Iowa: Parsons Technology, 1998.

Vine, W. E., Merrill F. Unger, and William White, Jr. *Vine's Expository Dictionary of Old and New Testament Words.* Chattanooga, Tennessee: AMG Publishers, 1996.

5433 - 6018 - 0990 - 0924
01126
752 CV

CPSIA information can be obtained at www.ICGtesting.com
Printed in the USA
LVOW10s1851100515

437958LV00001B/320/P